# The Director Of School Music

# The Director Of School Music

by

JOHN PAUL JONES, PH. D.

Head, Department of Music
*Delta State College*

Cleveland, Mississippi

DISTRIBUTORS
JENKINS MUSIC COMPANY
KANSAS CITY MO.

III

To

*Professor Charles B. Righter, director of bands, State University of Iowa, who first inspired me with the possibilities and responsibilities of teaching music in the public schools.*

JOHN PAUL JONES

IV

# FOREWORD

An attempt to increase the already long list of music books might seem futile but for one fact: the subject of this book, the director of school music, has been neglected far out of proportion to the attention placed on the medium through which he works—the printed music and the groups which reproduce it. Practically nothing has been written about the director as an individual and as a potent factor in the development of his field.

The purpose of this writing is to focus attention on the director of music, his problems and their solutions. The older and more experienced director will find oft forgotten phases brought to his attention; the younger director, striving valiantly for higher performing and organization standards, will find help and encouragement; and to all is given a comfortable sharing of school music problem solutions.

The educational approach which surely must be adopted by the director of music is so ably summed up in the thoughts of the dedicatee who feels that, except in the field of serious professional performance, music's classification as one of the fine arts has been more of a hope than a reality. The hope that it may achieve its rightful stature in the amateur field can only become a reality when teachers generally appreciate the importance of combining musical knowledge, technical skill, and the artistic self-expression in the finished product. Neglect or carelessness in any of these areas can only reduce musical performance to an absurd and meaningless activity.

Music directors, as educators, must emphasize the importance of building a musical structure which is practical, durable, and artistic. Upon a solid foundation of musical theory, must be a superstructure in which the elements of utility and beauty are the most prominent features. While technical display should not overshadow musical content, technical inadequaces should never stand in the way of interpretation.

Finally, he feels it is the teacher's responsibility to develop equally, and concurrently, all of the intellectual, technical,

V

and emotional elements essential to musical performance. To do this properly, the teacher of music must take advantage of every possible aid to the enrichment of his own technical and artistic resources.

It is hoped the reader will accept this book in accordance with the above and in the light of actual teaching experiences and problem solutions which, in reality, it is.

The author is indebted to his wife, Margaret, and to Rose Marie Kaufman, for help in reading through the various chapters. Especially is he thankful for the splendid help given by his good friends Ruth and Ronald Gerard who so patiently read the finished manuscript, offering constructive and helpful suggestions. Lastly, the author appreciates the part played by his friends, directors and students, whose experiences, problems and solutions have been helpful in writing this book.

JOHN PAUL JONES

# CONTENTS

Chapter I

## INTRODUCTION

The art of producing fine musical organizations in the school is dependent on many very important factors not the least of which is the director. There have been many theses on the production of music and musical experiences but little attention has been given the director in relationship to the other factors so vital in the production of good music. The musician of long experience already has a deep feeling for, and a sympathetic understanding of, the many problems which confront the music director—a great many of which will be emphasized and discussed in this book from the standpoint of the successful director.

There is no intention here to tell or show any director how to do his work nor to place a high standard before him with the proposal that it be reached else he shall fail as a director of music. Such is not the object of this book. Neither is it intended to be fantastic nor trite for if the many topics under discussion are fantastic then the school music program is fantastic and if the content be trite it is because the degree of these *common* things show a need for more usable knowledge. Wide experience has proven the worth of these forth-coming topics of discussion and time will justify the value of their application in the direction of school music programs.

Such a program of school music as has been developed in the United States can hardly be called fantastic, nor can it be encouraged and supported by processes called trite. While this book will not bring new and startling processes for developing bands, orchestras and choral groups, it does intend to focus greater attention on the necessary fundamentals from which we often stray. A sincere effort is being made to emphasize those things which make better musical organizations. Individual and group problems are exposed and suitable remedial methods are proposed.

### What Price Value?

The value of any school organization is measured by the amount of dependence placed in it by the school program as a whole. It might be well for the music director to make a critical analysis of his musical organiztions in the light of their true worth as judged with unbiased opinion. Many questions may present themselves: does the band, orchestra, or choral group, as an educational organization, deserve such intensive training as is sometimes given it? Must the musical organization, from an educational standpoint, be treated in a way different from other class or school organizations? Is there an advantage for the the music student over the non-music student? Is a school, which emphasizes one musical organization to the detriment of others, meeting the need? Sometimes the true value of musical organizations is overlooked in the midst of biased opinion. Surely it is agreed that the sole purpose of school music is not the production of a marching band alone, a concert band only or, in the case of vocal music, the production of a single trio or quartet. The least of the purposes of school music organizations should be the contest for the sake of winning. The winning of a school music contest should come as an aftermath of good training and productive enterprize rather than as the sole purpose for the existence of the organization.

## Lack of Traditional Foundation

Intensive training of music students often seems more intensive than it really is. Other high school subjects have a well organized elementary and junior high school teaching-background of several years before they are taught on the high school level. Ordinarily, music does not have this. Mathematics, English, history and other traditional subjects are taught, in some form, through all the grades. When the student has reached the high school level, the teacher has a pupil fairly well steeped in the traditional subjects. This is not so with the high school music field especially in the instrumental phase. The tradition in music has become, then, that the teacher of high school music must do musically in three or four years what the academic subject teachers do over a period of nine to twelve years. Thus the music work in the secondary school has the appearance of being highly intensified when, by rights, a great amount of the study is for the purpose of teaching what should have been taught years earlier.

The high school teacher of traditional academic subjects has a whole corp of assistants back down in the grades who build the foundation on which rests the high school work but not so with the high school director of music. *He has to do the whole thing himself!* In other words, one man is expected to do in a few years with music what we patiently wait for over a long period of time in the academic subjects. The miraculous thing is that music directors are doing this very thing year after year and doing it successfully. It might be stated further that were academic subjects treated in a manner similar to music, the academic level of our schools would surpass even the fondest of dreams.

## Values and Objectives

The value of fine school music organizations is two-fold: they afford a means of self expression for the child who takes a playing or singing interest, and for the non-playing or non-singing student they act as an aid to a better understanding and a better appreciation for music. Thus appreciation and discrimination are taught through participation in music either by listening to it or by producing it, or by a combination of both.

There can be no objection to some intensive training in music for it is necessary in any subject where a thorough, workable foundation is to be laid. This is especially true where time is a factor. The first endeavor in teaching music is to help the child to become a good appreciator and a good discriminator of music; that he may learn to listen intelligently, and criticize intelligently the music he hears. The lack of a thorough musical training can not be excused on the grounds that we are not turning out professional musicians. The young student trained in a careless manner will develop into a careless listener for he learned not how to listen nor for what to listen. How well the great mass of listening material, such as recordings and radio programs, is put to good use depends in a large measure on the school music director. Human beings simply can not appreciate something about which they know nothing.

It is the purpose of the following chapters to touch on many of the fundamentals so necessary to achieve desirable goals in music participation.

Chapter II

## MUSICAL STANDARDS

Any school music organization which can meet the standards of district, state and national contests has a right to distinction. Even an attempt to meet these standards shows aggressiveness and a desire to lift the organization to the highest level possible. The director is always interested in the exact processes so necessary in attaining these goals yet how can one strive for these standards without knowing for what to work? The answer to this question had its beginning in a thorough study of many contest reports written by state and national judges. An investigation of these reports reveals that a few major factors are necessary and requisite to a desirable performance: intonation, tone quality, phrasing, rhythm, interpretation, tempo, technique and general effect.

Each one of these factors may well be treated individually in the rehearsal but when it comes to fine group performance they cease to be individual points and become one composite whole. In other words, what is heard is not the separate and individual musical elements but the result of a judicious mixing of the whole in such proportions as to result in a splendid and laudable performance. When this performance falters in any respect then the composite whole must be broken down and the exact trouble located. It may be any one of the above factors, or perhaps several of them.

### Intonation

Good intonation is possible only when the players have the proper conception of pitch relationships; that is, the tone distance of one note from the other.

Players should be taught to tune not by comparing note to note but by listening for the *beat*. By way of instrumental example, let one player sound the note on a trumpet then another trumpet player sound the same note with the tuning slide pulled out a little. Now, if the two notes are sounded at the same time there will be a decided waving or pulsating beat set up between the two tones. This may not be noticed by all the students until attention is called to it. Now have the player, who has previously pulled out the tuning slide, gradually push the slide in while the two notes are being sounded. As the slide is pushed in notice that the *beating* (fighting between the two notes) becomes slower and slower. When the two notes are exactly in tune there will be no beat at all. Piano, organ and, in fact, all tuning is done by this method. It is fascinating to the music student and he soon becomes very adept in understanding its application. This tuning fact is a splendid application of a physics problem in acoustics and might well be correlated with similar work in the physics department, a procedure in no way frowned upon by the pursuants of educational policies.

The next step, after good tuning, is to practice scales and arpeggios, learning the musical distance of all the intervals from a second to an octave. Some students do so little of this kind of practice that, when asked to play the upper octave of a note, they have been known to play almost a tone flat. The only reason being that they do not understand how the octave should sound. They know the fingering but not the sound. Octave practice is indispensible. After octave practice there should follow practice on the fourths, fifths, thirds, sixths and other intervals. This interval practice will show results in chord practice which, in turn, will pay dividends in concert playing. In making corrections, it is better to let the student or students analyze the fault and suggest the correction, being guided by the director, of course. To do so keeps them "pitch-minded." By learning to analyze and suggest corrections in the work of others, the players will soon learn to analyze and correct their own playing faults. No organization becomes a good sounding organization until each member learns to listen carefully to the musical notes played by his neighbor.

Knowledge of intervals and how they sound are no less valuable to the vocal student than to the instrumental. In fact, a keen knowledge of tone-distance is even more important to vocal students because there are no mechanical devices to help locate the tone as the instrumentalist has in the keyed instrument. Therefore, the value of interval practice can not be over stressed to any student of music, vocal or instrumental.

## Tone Quality

Nothing improves tone quality better, or quicker, than practice on long tones whether it be a vocal group or an instrumental group. Some directors spend a few minutes of each rehearsal on long tones. This is laudable, but a greater success is assured when the singer or player learns the value of such procedure during his individual daily practice. Repeated long tones, stressing equal tone quality each time, will also increase tonal flexibility. Crescendos and diminuendos on one note, with attention to an even tone color and an even pitch, is also excellent practice whether it be by the individual or by the group. Instrumentally, lip slurs serve as excellent practice for building up the tone quality. The same effect is obtained vocally by singing (vocalizing) simple slurred intervals.

## Phrasing

Quite often an organization seems to lose sight of the true value of phrasing and some play or sing as if there were no such thing at all. In other words, the little curved line over or under a group of notes is practically meaningless. The beauty gained by properly phrasing a musical passage can not be over stressed. All notes enclosed under a phrasing indication should be so played, the musical effect depending upon the correctness of the playing. A common fault is to allow the phrase to *play out* toward the end. Sometimes the phrase pattern is completely ignored not only by individual players or singers within a section but by the entire section, thus the general effect is that is dis-organization. The value of good phrasing or any phrasing at all is entirely lost if all do not phrase their particular part exactly in a uniform manner. Good phrasing may be developed, as may also a knowledge of the relationship of melody and accompaniment, if some time is spent on simple songs. No better material exists for this purpose than folk songs, church tunes or chorales.

## Breathing

A common statement is that good phrasing means good breathing. As a matter of fact, the reverse is more nearly true; good breathing means good phrasing. Much of the phrasing problem has been solved when good breathing habits are taught. Oft-times the student will complain of running out of breath. Such a condition is a natural one unless correct breathing is understood and practiced. Good breathing does not mean to wait until the lungs have been completely emptied before taking a fresh breath. There may be times when the reserve amount of breath seems quite adequate yet good breathing and good phrasing would require a fresh supply. Often the young student will get an entirely new conception of melodic line merely through better breathing habits which result in better phrasings.

It is normal to breathe with the top part of the lungs *only* when speedy use of the breath allows for no more lung action. Singing and instrumental playing does not often require this speed therefore using the full lung capacity affords complete mastery of the wind supply problem. The common expression for full lung breathing is *abdominal breathing*. There is no mystery here: the term means merely to breathe with the lower half of the lungs as well as with the upper half, as witness: the natural breathing of the sleeping person, or the breathing of the cat or dog when asleep. The student will do well to practice breathing, using the lower half of the lungs only. A better exercise would be: (1) fill the top half of the lungs (2) fill the lower half of the lungs (3) exhale from the top half of the lungs only (4) exhale from the lower half and (5) repeat the process several times daily.

## Rhythm

Observation has shown that many choral groups, bands and orchestras have poor rhythm because they either do not feel or do not understand the underlying pulse of the composition Some students are endowed by nature with a feeling for rhythm; some must develop their feeling for it. An established feeling for the first beat in every measure will go a long way toward a better rhythmic understanding by the entire organization. Rhythm exercises are not too elementary for any group, be it non-professional or professional. An excellent way to develop a feeling for the first beat of each measure is to sing or play only the note on beat one, counting out the balance of the measure and coming in again on the first beat of the next measure. Another way to help develop a rhythmic feeling for the first beat in each measure is to play or sing the melody by omitting every other measure, that is: omit every second, fourth, sixth measure etc. To come in on the right beat, the student must keep an accurate account of the silent measure value. After some practice in this manner, try it out by having the entire organization play or sing every first, third, fifth measure and so on. To elaborate on this, have certain sections sing measures one, three, five etc., while other sections sing only measures two, four, six etc.

Rhythm must dove-tail horizontally. When it is time for the first beat all must be ready for the first beat, not the last half of it nor the eighth before, but right on it. Playing a number by leaving out every other measure or every third measure also encourages strict attention to the printed page and eliminates the tendency of some to "ride" on the ability of others.

### Rhythm by Phrases

Take a simple song of the folk-song type which is phrased by a two or four measure grouping and let the organization do one phrase, understanding that it is a complete thought. Then continue on to the next thought. Soon the ensemble will have a good understanding of the rhythm by phrases as well as a good understanding of measured rhythm. Organizations which sight read poorly often make almost unbelievable advancement in reading as soon as there is established a feeling for the first beat of every measure and the first beat of every phrase. To be sure this is elementary but, frankly, many of our musical organizations need more of the elementary things.

### Interpretation

Let the director stray not too far from the accepted interpretation of standard numbers if an example of the standard interpretation is available. Good and accepted interpretations of most of the well known standard members can be learned from phonograph records, both vocal and instrumental— and especially the latter. When playing or singing a number not of the old standard type, the interpretation should be that of good taste. A personal peculiarity of taste should not interfere with the interpretation unless there is excellent reason to back it up.

No director has a license to his own interpretation simply because he is the director. Although this attitude is sometimes taken, it should never be used as a shield to cover a lack of musical common sense. A director, in a national band contest, used a number around which had grown a traditional interpretation. But this director had worked out his own interpretation and was so sure of it and made it so musical that the adjudicator, in this case a nationally known band director, wrote: "I can not agree with your interpretation which is not the accepted interpretation but your band did a splendid job with an instrumentation keen in detail." This adjudicator gave the band a first division rating with compliments.

Whatever the interpretation be, let it ring of true musicianship with reasonableness and discretion in its use. Do not lean to radical interpretations for they may be neither reasonable nor musical. A good interpretation should be musically likable to those who listen to it: not to the man on the podium especially but to the audience.

Not only should the traditional interpretation be studied but close attention should be paid to the meaning of the Italian words indicating tempos, dynamics, expression, etc. Another help in interpretation is making good use of metronomic markings and finally, the conductor's own sense of musicianship.

## Tempo

Tempo has much in common with interpretation. There are acceptable tempos at which certain passages of standard numbers should be taken. Normally, any deviation is to be frowned upon yet at times the opposite is quite acceptable: that no passage be attempted at a rate of speed faster than it can be well played.

Instrumentally, it is much more musical to play a passage within the speed limits of the players and do it musically than to attempt to reach the indicated or accepted speed if it is far beyond the ability of the musicians. Such attempts often lead to a conglomerated unmusical mess. The vocalist is more fortunate in this respect for pronounciation and enunciation are rather accurate gauges to decent tempos.

The proper tempo other than that limited by player ability may be determined in several ways, through:

1. Melodic line, whether the key be major or minor; rapidity of notes or sustained tones; rugged or dulcet in quality and so on.

2. general terms usually marked on the score such as allegro, vivace, presto, etc.

3. exact metronomic markings, easily noted and usually at the beginning of each movement.

4. traditional conception of tempo obtained by listening to professional organizations or their recordings, and

5. the basic underlying pulse which does not change as the theme changes but rather controls the "flow" of the music.

It is not always possible to have the same playing pulse in concert or contest as is experienced in rehearsal. Therefore, the wise director will have trained himself to sense the "pulse" of the performing organization and to do so quickly. Some days the organizations can do all passages at a very rapid tempo; on other days this speed may be lessened considerably. Quick adaptation of the director to the performing mood of the group will not only lessen the strain on the director, but will increase the bond between him and the ensemble. Too many times the performance is below par because the director is fighting the musicians with tempo. The art of sensing the mood of the organization as a whole during a performance is indeed a valuable one. Furthermore, there is always the possibility that the ensemble is normal and it is the director who has changed. It is much easier to adapt one man to a group than to adapt the group to the man and the thinking director will understand the full meaning of this.

### Technique

Technique is considered important but not to the extent of placing it above all else. Technique without beautiful and expressive playing or singing has little compensation. On the other hand, the player should be able to "get over the keys" with plenty of agility when the part so requires and the singer should be equally well versed in vocal passages. The speed at which a number may be taken is limited by the technique of the player but technique is a friend indeed if, when playing at a reasonable speed, the player experiences the thrill of intricate passages correctly played. Practice on arpeggios, on passages requiring awkward fingerings, thirds, fourths and fifths in various keys will give the fingers plenty of exercise mechanically. Technique should be perfected to the point where the player forms the habit of playing the passage without the labor of thinking them through.

The drummer has a standard series of twenty-six rudiments most of which are indispensable. There are *flams* which compare to grace notes; *five stroke rolls* which compare to four extremely short notes before a long note; the *long roll* which is a series of short notes executed so rapidly that there appears to be a continuous sound. All these, and many more, illustrate the fine organization of the routine of drumming technique. When the drummer sees a series of notes he does not study whether it be a paradiddle or a flamacue—*he plays it before he thinks,* so well has he drilled himself in technical fundamentals. The same should be true of players on other instruments. Passages easy in one key may be difficult in another, therefore the wise director will encourage the practice of transposing passages into various keys. By playing the same passage in different keys, new fingering problems come to light and the mastery of these develops agility to an amazing degree.

There are many methods which develop technique primarily but if plenty of arpeggio practice in various keys, and a good foundation of scales and interval studies seems absolutely necessary for the professional, it is even more necessary to the young amateur.

## General Effect

General effect is the sum total of all the good and bad in the organization as reflected in the eyes, ears and mind of the listener. If an organization has qualities which are so good as to far outweigh and outnumber the inferior, it is immediately called a first class organization. On the contrary, if the inferior qualities outnumber and outweigh the good, the group is relegated to a much lower plane. This manner of rating a musical organization, be it for contest or concert purposes, is perfectly fair. Any organization which has good rhythm, tempo, tone, and renders a musical interpretation with ample technique, will produce a fine, pleasing and satisfying general effect—a one-plus rating regardless of the purpose of performance.

Among the factors which help to create the general effect is *musical discipline*. Not the kind of discipline which has to do with group behavior (although this is an item) but a kind of discipline which produces musical results, that is: (1) close attention to each individual part which, in turn, results in (2) good reading, and (3) good posture which indicates an interest in the appearance of the organization as well as the improvement in playing. A slouchy posture of the player or singer never produces a good effect on a listener and crossed knees never indicates a musical genius. Neither does leaning on the instrument or the neighboring musician.

## Rhythm—Head or Foot

The patting of feet should be eliminated as far as association with concert playing or singing is concerned. There are those who advocate it as an aid to good rhythm but few, if any, will condone its use in concert appearances. For two reasons foot patting should be eliminated: first, it is not really necessary musically. The player should train himself to think the rhythm; not only to *think* the rhythm but to *feel* it just as automatically as when he presses the valves or keys to make the notes. Second, the patting of feet is a very unsightly affair from the viewpoint of the audience. Some pat with the toes, some with the heel and some will alternate heel and toe. It is well to remember that the eyes of the audience are usually just about level with the floor of the stage or performing platform. From this point, the feet are very noticable especially when in motion. At first, the moving feet are somewhat disconcerting: soon it becomes amusing and finally reaches the ridiculous stage. Let such a distraction be held in abhorance. Better still, concentrate on some good basic replacement for this "foot-rhythm" with which so many groups are afflicted.

Chapter III

THE DIRECTOR, HIS NECESSARY BACKGROUND

The music director is normally expected to be well versed in the music subjects which he or she teaches. There is no reason to think otherwise. The state requirements for teaching music usually see that the academic part of the musical education is taken care of and, fortunately, these requirements for certification are gradually being raised to a higher level. The present-day director has every opportunity to be trained well enough to meet not only the state requirements but also the requirements of the particular school which employs him, and the requirements of the community in which he works.

With all the "book knowledge" possible for the director to accumulate, he is still far from holding the requisites of a good director if he does not possess a genuine love for his chosen work. More than this, he must be happy not only in his work but happy in the place where he is working. The greatest compensation is not in dollars and cents although the pay is usually good. But, the teaching of music is filled with thrills and fascination found only in the unraveling of musical knots and tangles. The growth of eagerness and enthusiasm in the young players and singers is always noticable. When the director becomes their idol and they hope to some day become a musician and teacher like him, monetary reward is quickly forgotten.

But the director must become a little selfish. While he or she is striving earnestly to build the organizations and to instill new musical life into young musicians, the director must take "time out" to raise his own musical level and to better prepare himself for the work to come. This kind of selfishness is perfectly justifiable for in building himself he will, in turn, build better music in the schools. The college courses, so universally requisite to teaching, should never be considered final; they are no more final than the periodic predictions that the world is coming to an end. The all too small amount of musical education available in the four-year college course should be considered only as a foundation on which to build a greater musical knowledge; it is only a challenge to learn more. Those who take advantage of the challenge will forge ahead. Those who fail to realize the possibilities based on the four-year college course will remain right where the four-year course puts them.

One thing is quite positive: the director must assume all responsibility for the outcome of the musical effects produced by his organization. The director need not alibi if the instrumentation is below par; he need not complain if the compositions are seemingly below the quality for such as his own organization providing the numbers are well performed. Certainly no complaints should be in order if the size is small providing the result is musically acceptable. Small organizations should sing and play in pitch as well as large organizations do. Size alone does not control intonation. There should be no difference in phrasing, tonguing, dynamics or other factors just because the band, orchestra or chorus is small.

Instrumentally, large organizations will surely have a better proportion of tone color—that would naturally be assumed, but size alone will not produce a good band, orchestra, chorus or any other musical organization. Good playing is not dependent on large numbers. In fact, quite the oposite is true. The author remembers quite distinctly the disappointment felt when he expected to hear a splendid bit of playing from a high school band of one hundred and eight pieces. Coming down the street nine abreast and with a stirring cadence, all expectations were to hear a fine street march but hopes were shattered when the first measure was blasted forth. How much wiser it would have been to have eliminated half the players and thus have relieved the band of half the "blue notes." The band was seriously handicapped by being numerically strong. It would have been infinitely better had the poorer players been eliminated entirely or, perhaps, appeared latter in the parade as an intermediate or junior band. The quality of the first band would thus be improved and the second band could have used music suitable to its ability. No doubt, in the latter case, the showing of both would have been exceptionally commendable.

Too often the director will apologize for the smallness of the chorus, band or orchestra but a small group can perform just as well in tune as a large one. The attacks, releases and dynamics can be just as fine as that of the large groups for the mechanics of good performance can be applied to any group of any size.

Just how much of a musical foundation is necessary to good teaching is quite debatable and certainly the director's ability to teach other academic subjects is no criterion for his selection as a teacher in the field of music.

### Musical Feeling

First, the director should be endowed, by nature, with a general sense of musical feeling. He should have a natural feeling for rhythm. Without a good sense of rhythm, the director is musically marooned from the start since rhythm is one of the basic fundamentals of music. The director should have a natural feeling for dynamic contrasts and musical phrasing, the very essence of which makes music *live* in the hands of one director and die in the hands of another who lacks that feeling. He should have a feeling for pitch and necessary tempo changes, ritards, accelerandos, holds, etc. Couple this with an understanding of the accepted interpretations and the result should be, for the most part, a fairly good background for reasonable, acceptable conducting.

But even without these musical senses inborn to a marked degree, the director can become successful if he or she has the ability to work everlastingly on the methods of teaching music, interpretations through recordings, and other pertinent and timely musical problems. All of this is, of course, in addition to a good thorough study of music history, appreciation, the various studies included in music theory, and other related subjects in the field of music.

### Instrumental Knowledge

It is quite necessary that the director have a good working knowledge of each family of instruments and preferably of each individual instrument although it would be quite foolish to expect the director to be a proficient performer on every instrument. Most every band or orchestra director, with his working knowledge of the various instruments, might, with practice, become a competent performer on any instrument but no one should expect the director to be a soloist on all instruments. He has greater work to do. His job ceased to be that of artist-performer when he became a teacher of others.

A knowledge of the tone-color of every instrument is necessary as is also a knowledge of the tone-color resulting when two or more of the instrumental tones are blended, whether they be of the same or different families. It should be borne in mind that the tone-color reaching the audience is the objective rather than the tone-color as it is actually heard by the director at close range. The wise director soon learns to translate the tone colors he hears into that which the audience receives. In other words, the director must listen as if he were quite some distance back of himself.

The director must sense the dynamic balance of his organization as it sounds when it reaches the audience for as a rule the sound heard in the auditorium is quite different from that heard on the stage. He must be aware that double-forte in some passages for some instruments—brasses, for instance, could not be matched by a double-forte in the woodwinds. Conversely, a pianissimo in the woodwinds is most difficult to match with the brass. To sense this difference in dynamic levels of instruments and instrumental families makes for finer conducting and finer results regardless of whether the director has the sense of tonal balance, God-given in the fullest, or has found it necessary to develop a meager portion of it to the Nth degree.

### Insight

The director must have, either native or acquired, that *something* which gives him an insight to musical thought and expression—he must have a *feel* for the way it should go. Not only must he have this but he must be able to communicate his ideas to the performer in a plain and clear-cut manner.

The director has a complicated task. He must see and hear the composition in its completed form and then pass on to the musicians his conception of the composer's intention. In turn, he is responsible for the passing of this conception, through the performers, on to the listening public. The director must do this in a vigorous and positive manner. If he fails to impress his group in a positive way, he quite naturally has failed to impress his listeners, and he has lessened his possibilities as a successful director.

### Standards

As to musical standards, the director must catch all rebuffs from his performers, his listening public, and himself. First of all, he must meet his own standards as nearly as possible but he must alter or adjust these standards to meet the ability of his group and then adjust the entire standard thus far gained to meet the standards of the listening public, although the standards may be below those desired by the director. This brings up the age-old question as to whether the director should play *down* to the audience or *up* to his own standard. After all, a little broadminded thinking will show the reasonableness of gradually edging in with music of a higher calibre by first gaining attention through that music which the public best understands. Again, let it be remembered that one can not appreciate what one does not understand. One mission of the good director is to cultivate and enlarge on the musical tastes of his public as he himself develops. All tastes can be satisfied easily if a varied program is followed and this, in itself, is good directorship. As the audience becomes more discriminating, the standard of the program may become higher.

The answer to a great many of these problems comes only through experience and each bit of experience helps to make a better musical background which is necessary for continued good work. Listening to as many musical organizations as possible is very beneficial especially if the director will make mental or written notes of the general musical effects gained. Other activities of value include the observation of music classes under the direction of other music teachers; the reading of books and magazine articles of musical nature; listening to records and radio programs. All of these, plus the continued experience of actual directing, will build a musical background such as will vault any obstacle that may present itself.

Chapter IV

## THE DIRECTOR'S PERSONALITY

The influence of the music director on young musicians is probably stronger and more lasting than is generally understood. What must a music director have in order to create this feeling? To be sure, the director who uses iron-fisted methods may produce a fine mechanical organization but he would hardly be called a successful director since musical results are only a part of the many by-products of a good education for most students. The pleasing, dynamic personality is always to be preferred over the two-fisted, hard-boiled variety.

### What Is Personality

Personality is difficult to explain. It is much easier to say what personality is not than to say what it is. We are quick to remark about the pleasing personality of a person yet we are slow to define the qualities we see or sense in that person. A good conductor must be a composite of all the things good admired by the students who work for him. Now, junior and senior high school students may not always be bright but they are incessantly smart. They will "spot" the weaknesses and strengths of the teacher quicker than all the psychological tests rolled into one. The point here is that the teacher, in this case the director of music, must learn to capitalize on every possibility given him by the Great Maker which tends toward being a human being better liked by the students. The good director will suppress that side of his nature which is quick to find fault without due cause; he will suppress that side of his nature which is easily irritated; he will suppress that side of his nature which makes him work and fret over some set-back or reverse when that time could be better spent figuring out the correction. Generally, systematized thinking will be a priceless asset to the personality of the director.

### Appearance

The first impression of the director is usually gained through *sight*, being most often seen before he is heard. Therefore appearance is important.

It is not intended that the director should be a "Hollywood Stylist"—far from it, but to a great extent the old saying: "Fine feathers make fine birds" may well be applied to the director. The students want to see their director well groomed, immaculately clean and neat when he appears before them. They have a right to want this.

It is quite impossible not to create some kind of an impression on the students so why not endeavor to create the most desirable impression possible. Why not watch such things as shined shoes, neckties to match the shirt which, in turn, should match the suit which, in turn should be well pressed at all times. Now these are little things individually, but they are a pretty big figure in the sum total. It is not necessary to put a large financial outlay in clothes. Generally, that is impossible. So, additional clothing should be purchased with the idea of matching that already at hand. If a complete new outfit is to be purchased, then have it well matched using good taste as to color, style and service. A blue necktie does not go with a brown suit nor a brown shirt with a blue serge suit. It takes only a few moments to clear the dust of yesterday's parade off the shoes. Neatness and harmony in what is worn are far more important than the style being worn.

Being of the male sex, it is much easier (and safer) to talk about the men but feminine friends will admit that an attractive dress suitable to the complexion and physical form of the wearer will command far more respect from the student than will a hodge-podge of ill-chosen frills. Choose decorations wisely and carefully. Try not to wear a "manish" or tailored outfit. If a sports outfit suits your personality and general make-up best, then by all means wear it. In other words, take what the Good Being gave you and build upon that native personality. If your hair is red don't resign yourself to the fact that you must always wear green or brown. Take advantage of the gift of nature which makes it almost impossible for you to go wrong in selecting an admirable outfit.

### Voice

Personal appearance alone is not enough. Next to being

*seen* the director is usually heard. Therefore, the director should develop a pleasing voice which should be well modulated even though there are times when this seems quite impossible. In speaking, the manner should be convincing and sincere, and in quality and quantity should suit the occasion for which it is used. Try to develop a good conversational tone—not one of a sing-song, monotonous clatter. The voice should rise and fall in keeping with the meaning of the words and it should carry all inflection necessary to impart a dramatic feeling or dramatic touch to the thought expressed. Good pronunciation and clear enunciation are always desirable, and even more so when speaking in a large room. Speaking the word correctly and saying the syllables clearly is more effective than raising the pitch of the voice.

## Smile

One should cultivate a smile if not endowed with one by nature. The smile should be on duty at all times even in face of a musical disaster. An honest-to-goodness smile, encouraging at all times and sympathetic when necessary, is indespensible. Nobody loves a scolder. Students soon become calloused to the constant scolder, and the threats of a scolding director soon become meaningless. There is nothing more encouraging to the young student than a cheery good-morning smile or, at the end of the day, a friendly good-bye. The ability to smile is a most valuable asset and it probably occupies the greater part of this thing called personality. There is no place in music for the unkind, unfriendly director who makes a show of losing his temper, topping it off with scolding words and the throwing of batons.

## Poise

In addition to a pleasing appearance and a pleasant voice the director has need for poise. Students quickly sense ungraceful movements, becoming ill at ease before the awkward director. One should cultivate relaxation as an aid to walking gracefully and easily, and even as an aid to stepping to and from the podium as well as every other movement before the group. Oftimes this awkwardness is caused solely by nervous tension. But, one who is capable of directing a band, orchestra or chorus, and is given that confidence by the school administration when hired for the job, has little cause for an outward appearance of tension or awkwardness.

## Tact

The director should endeavor to cultivate a form of tact most suitable to, and workable through, his own peculiar nature. Some directors handle situations with one tactful procedure which to others would be useless. The approach taken by the director is dependent upon the reaction of his nature to the situation at hand together with the group reaction of those concerned. Tact depends on the type of a person you are and the type of students with which you are working. It becomes necessary, then, to study the situation carefully and oftimes quickly so that only one decision is necessary and final. It is not good tact to have to back down on a decision, but it is good tact to admit an honest mistake. "Face-saving" must not be confused with tact. The director had best be right first and be able to back up his statements in some manner with facts. To be able to do so requires an understanding with the administration as to policy and the limits of the director's jurisdiction.

Tact does not imply blunt answers. People like to hear even harsh things said in a pleasant manner. You can prove a person wrong and make him like it if you do not make him angry in the process of so doing. But, if he does become angry and you have the ability to get him in a good humor again, you not only have tact—you are a diplomat!

The director must be openminded to suggestions from every source and no greater opportunity for displaying tact arises than when making decisions on these suggestions. Many of the suggestions will be utterly useless and many of them which appear usable will, when tried, prove impractical but the artful application of tact will avoid many a delicate situation and possibly some bright, workable idea will come to light—even, perhaps, from a parent.

## Humor

Lastly, the director MUST have a sense of humor. Do not think for even a minute that this implies a lack of sincerity in teaching music. Not at all! The teaching of music must be taken seriously but not to the extent of letting it become a hazard to good work. Neither should one try to become a comedian, and, least of all, try to "wise-crack" through the class hour. Such procedure only lessens the director in the eyes of the young musicians. Unless the director can be constantly original and extremely clever in the presentation of his comic material, he had better not try. If he can be constantly original and extremely clever, he has missed his calling. However, many a serious incident and many a tense rehearsal can be smoothed out through the judicious use of humor.

Chapter V

# THE DIRECTOR PLANS HIS ORGANIZATION.

The finest relationship will exist between the music director and his students when the director regards them as an intricate part of a fine musical organization of which he, too, is a co-worker for the good of the whole. Such a feeling on the part of all brings a healthy response through affection and respect for both the director and the music.

The duties of the school music director may be divided into two categories: first, the general organization and, second, the actual conducting. The problems confronting the director as an organizer will be brought to light for while the ability to organize a group is commendable, to do so in a constructive way is paramount. Too many inexperienced music directors feel that some knowledge of band, orchestra and choral music and some contact with related teaching methods is the only essential thing. Perhaps this comes from the very fact that experience alone magnifies the need for more than academic study.

There are several plans of organizing the school music program. Actually, plans work in as many ways as there are directors practicing them. Only a few will be discussed for most plans are closely, if not directly, related to these few. In general practice, the plan of organization usually ranges from the hit-and-miss to the highly complicated type of music promotion. The former has few, if any, definite steps leading to participation in the first or "top" music organization while the latter may be a definite long-range program from the beginning to the final stages of perfection.

## Direct Individual Advancement

One plan is that of direct entrance into the advanced chorus, band or orchestra through private instruction of some sort. Too often this plan results from an already over crowded workday where no time is allowed the director for class instruction in music during school hours. He is, therefore, required to teach privately outside of the regular school day if he is to accomplish anything. Again, in some instances, the director is required to earn part of his salary in this manner, supplementing his school pay with private lesson remuneration. In such case, the administration seems to expect the honor and glory of having the school musical organization but refuses to accept the financial responsibility which goes with it. This generally relates to the school where the director of music must be in the unfortunate situation of teaching subjects other than music. Such greatly handicaps the music program, or prevents any at all.

The glory of the above system is that the music director achieves the success he does under the handicaps—success attributed in the main to the ability of the director rather than to the cooperation of all other factors concerned. What his achievements might be with proper schedules and administrative backing may well be guessed.

Another direct advancement plan has been applied quite successfully in some towns. While similar to the above, the principle difference in results achieved seems to be in the application of the method. The most successful use of this system requires an instruction book for each individual by which the student masters certain lessons and reaches certain achievements each week, the advancement being marked or checked off and the student then given an advance assignment in accordance with the progress made. This is individual advancement, and progress is often much faster than where instruction is given in group fashion. Certainly the young players have knowledge of the exact requirements each week, and also have the advantage of the personal attention of the teacher. Being able to meet each student personally is the strength of this system but it does require a tremendous amount of organization and teacher time.

The time requirement is one of the chief objections. The director is kept busy seeing and hearing the young players, constantly marking their achievements and giving assignments. This is not really in the form of a private lesson but merely enough time is given to adjudicate the work of the student. The advantage lies in the director's complete knowledge of the ability of every student. However, this individual checking enables the director to pass on many students during the week and it places considerable responsibility on the shoulders of the student.

## Group Teaching

There is some criticism passed on the individual system in that the student has little, if any, opportunity to grow in group experience, this coming to him only after he has made sufficient progress. The claim is that group teaching from the start gives the student an appreciation for group experience which carries on into the more advanced stages as he progresses.

A common method of teaching instrumental music is by classes of instrumental families, or instruments of like nature. Many band and orchestra directors think this is the ideal way in that it offers advantages in time saving, group learning and an enlarged participation. Some directors try to segregate the various instruments into classes of like instruments as nearly as possible; that is, they will try to have all trumpets at one time; all basses or baritones at one time, the strings or woodwinds at another. By this plan, every player is busy all the time. Explanations apply equally well to all players in each group. It is also advantageous in that players are always playing in registers suitable to their own particular instrument which is not always the case in a heterogenious grouping. It is easily seen that a group of basses can work together much better than could a group consisting of basses, flutes and horns.

The greatest objection to separate periods for like instruments is the lack of time available to accomodate all instrumental students. It may be that all cornets and trumpets can not meet at the cornet-trumpet hour thus one or more other cornet-trumpet hours must be scheduled. Perhaps the trombone section must be split, or the basses can not meet at the same time. This is a real handicap for the director who prefers to teach by such a plan but if the schedule permits, there is no doubt about the advisability of using it.

## Heterogenious Groupings

The third plan, and one quite widely used, is that of taking the instrumental class as they come, grouping any and all kinds of instruments as the students have vacant periods. While this plan may not be popular, it is probably most widely used for the very reason that many more students can be reached in some manner in less time. While the instruction which each child receives personally may be of a shorter duration, he is likely to receive that instruction more often and in relationship to group performance. There is no doubt but that this plan fits into the school schedule better than any other plan. It may entail some duplication of the instruction but this can not be helped and could well be considered an advantage. In many cases, a shift in the class schedule of a few students may eliminate the duplication altogether. One big advantage found in this plan is that young players learn group cooperation from the start. There is no loss in orientating the student to a new grouping of instruments when opportunity for advancement comes. All through the stages of instruction the players have learned to play in a mixed group; they have learned to appreciate tonal balance, dynamics, parts of contrary nature, and the value of an accompaniment. It seems advantageous to the student when he can be associated with this from the start as he is in a mixed group. When he graduates to the advanced organization he is not confronted with the sounds of new and strange instruments.

### Ensembles and Sectionals

One of the finest ways to develop a good band or orchestra is to encourage many ensemble groups. Too often a fine, large band will support only one brass quartet and one woodwind quartet; the orchestra supporting only one string quartet. There should be a great number of these smaller instrumental groups. Some directors build their top organizations around these smaller groups entirely. This is, indeed, a laudable procedure. One discouraging factor in promoting more small ensembles is the limit often placed on the number of these groups from any one town or city allowed to play in a contest. Generally, if a director does have several ensembles of the same instrumentation he can enter only one group in a contest. Quite naturally he enters the best of the lot. The only hope for the balance of the ensemble players is that something may happen to one of the top players thus requiring a substitute. Such a situation makes it almost hopeless for the third and fourth rate ensembles which this director has coached.

The solution of a fine ensemble approach lies in keeping the weaker groups playing as much as possible, making appearances where the level of their ability will suffice. Civic clubs, church meetings, school assemblies, home room programs, etc., all afford excellent opportunities for ensemble programs at various levels of perfection and ability. Perhaps the worst quartet in the senior high school would be a mighty source of inspiration to the junior high or grade school children. Something a little better may be necessary for the civic groups, allowing the best for the most discriminating audience. Thus, being fortified with more than one ensemble, the director can easily adjust the appearances to the need and ability and with less interruption of the school program as a whole. One of the greatest causes of friction between music and other departments is the constant absence of the same students from classes. A larger number of ensemble groups would solve this problem by spreading itself widely over the various other departments and no one teacher will have many absences chalked up against the music department.

## Private Lessons

In addition to the various methods of instrumental approach, the student can still take private lessons whether from the director or from some one outside the school. There is no substitute for the private teacher when it comes to detail which is sometimes lost in the teaching of large groups. To teach privately requires considerable time yet, aside from the additional revenue, the teacher is in a position to include teaching material pertinent to the work being done in the band or orchestra. To encourage this is to encourage and improve the playing of the performer and the performing group.

## Supplementary Material

Regardless of the teaching approach most acceptable to the director, it is very necessary that he have on hand at all times a supply of supplementary material which will bridge the gap between the beginning and the elementary, the elementary and the advanced. This supplementary material should cover a wide variety of studies so that regardless of the arising problem the proper corrective aid is at hand. Supplementary material should include not only scale studies in various forms but studies pertaining to phrasing, tonguing, rhythm, articulation and other necessary phases as may be necessary. Supplementary material should be more than a series of instruction books, it may include mimeographed sheets of fingering patterns, phrase patterns, slurring patterns etc. The development and advancement of the various players and groups will determine the need and the alert director will devise many supplementary things to meet his own need.

### Importance of Second and Third Parts

Students are often of the opinion that their instrument is of secondary importance. This is true especially in the horn section. the second and third cornets and clarinets and among the violas. In fact, most students who do not occupy first chairs or at least a first part have this feeling. One of the teaching problems in instrumental music is to create a feeling of importance among players on the inner parts. The ensemble can do much to aid in creating this feeling of importance for it comes as great joy to the players back on the last few chairs when they realize they can have a clarinet quartet just as do the fellows up on the front line. Playing third and fourth clarinet then ceases to require an apology and comes to life. Third and fourth part players soon realize they can have the same activity enjoyed by the first chair men, and they become more important to the organization because of it.

A member of the string quartet, brass or woodwind group, or any other ensemble soon learns to submerge his own individuality for the sake of the ensemble—a most necessary asset to good band and orchestra playing. The development of good ensembles may require a few extra hours of the instructor's time but there is no doubt about its value, and in time it will pay handsome dividends. No groups of high school students would be expected to do a splendid piece of work without help from the director, and the director should not expect them to. He may delegate to them the learning of the mechanics: the notes, rhythm and dynamics, but the true and finer interpretation must come from one who is more advanced than the players — the director.

## Holding Interest

The director able to have certain desirable material at hand when he needs it has gone far toward holding student interest. The fault, apparently, is in the lack of a variety of material in the school music library. There is a wealth of material on the market and the director able to have a good share of it is indeed fortunate. The less fortunate director must rely on the limits of his usually small budget. This director must then rely on his ingenuity and that of his students to increase individual interest.

Sometimes the director finds it necessary to sacrifice some of the aesthetic in order to reach a greater number of students. This is reasonable for in reaching a greater number of students he is also increasing the possibilities for a better selection of top players. By varying the requirements according to capabilities, experience and advancement, the director increases the student interest regardless of the level of learning. It is far better to teach the student to respect the art of playing musically than to try to force him into something beyond his capability and playing interest. Occasionally, forcing a student beyond his capability retards him rather than encourages him.

Another help in holding student interest is the matter of instrumentation. Ensemble instrumentation has become, generally, fairly well standardized but the director need not adhere strictly to the accepted grouping. In fact, there is much more to be learned by the student player if the grouping is a little out of proportion with itself. The accepted instrumentation for a string quartet is two violins, viola and cello. This should be the goal for string ensembles but there is no reason for not adding the string bass nor for doubling the size of the group.

Woodwind and brass groups may well be quite varied in instrumentation. Although the standard woodwind quintet consists of flute, oboe, clarinet, bassoon and French horn, there is no reason for not varying this considerably in young growing and training groups. As a matter of fact, the director will use *any* combination he can devise if it can be used as a training group. As the players grow in age and experience, the ensembles should round themselves into the more standardized instrumentations. One training group may furnish the nucleus for two or three ensembles of a more standardized nature. There is no better field for the teaching of unity and tonal balance, to say nothing of cooperation, than in the field of ensembles.

Suffice it to say that the director must think of his position as something greater than that of the music teacher alone. He, more than anyone else, holds the opportunity to instill the present-day youth with a belief in the values and beauty of music. In time these youths become the adult supporters of music. Certainly, the present-day director of music may not be the direct beneficiary but the music of tomorrow will benefit from his efforts. It might well be remembered that while the music director stops someday, music goes on and on forever.

Chapter VI

CONDUCTING

It has been said that Victor Hugo, when asked whether or not it was easy to write epic poetry, replied: "It is either easy or impossible." This might well apply to the music director as a conductor. Anyone may learn the simple matter of beating time but this happens to be only a small part of the many factors involved in conducting. Waving the baton is an easy matter but there is more "wollop" if it is done by a Toscanni, a Stokowskie or a Barbirolli than if done by you or I. Why is this? What does a nationally recognized conductor have that others have not? Any music department of a four-year college will offer a course in the fundamentals of conducting designed to teach the specific down and up beats, but there is no college course yet devised which will teach one how to *conduct*.

The director can not let himself be a stand-in for a metronome—he must become something more than a mere time-beater. The director must be the central point from which radiates direct lines of telepathic communication to the organization as a whole; to each separate section, and even to each individual when necessary. The director must be the controlling factor in every musical move, communicating this in some manner to the organization upon which he is "playing," be it chorus, band or orchestra. He must feel this communication between himself and the players, and the players must recognize the connection between themselves and the director. When this is done, the two factors, conductor and musicians, act as a unit in relation to the effect on the listening audience.

To get the most out of a performing group is the ultimate goal of the conductor yet the basic fundamentals necessary to achieve this goal are open to all and opportunities are plentiful. In the first place, the conductor must learn to sub-ordinate his own nature to that of controlling the feelings of his many performing musicians—no two of which are alike. No psychologist ever had a greater task than has the conductor who works with a group of high school or college students.

## Preparatory Steps

This business of conducting begins long before the rehearsal period as far as the school music groups are concerned. Some of these preparatory factors are: a clean room, properly placed chairs, music stands rightly placed if used, music folders in proper place, and all other needs properly attended to before rehearsal starts. In many cases the preparatory arrangements are taken care of by members of the organization—an admirable situation. In other cases the director does this himself. The latter seems a great waste of time but some directors feel it is the best method, and each to his own liking. In either case, it is up to the director to see that everything is in readiness for the rehearsal. A set-up ready for the students will go a long way to make them music minded quickly. There is a certain respect for an orderly rehearsal room, and one should make the most of it.

## Using the Baton

Assuming the director has had good training in the necessary fundamentals of conducting, he will have become acquainted with the use or non-use of the baton. Some instrumental directors prefer to use the baton and some do not. The same is true for the vocal directors. Since there is no rule, the conductor should feel free to use a baton or not use it as his mood and the need requires.

If the stick is to be used, try to hold it easily, naturally and comfortably yet with a firm grip and in such a manner that it is actually a continuation of the arm and hand. It is not advisable to hold it by the thumb and first finger only, nor is a club-like grip to be recommended. It should be used at an angle easily seen at all times by all members of the organization.

In conducting, the stick, and the left hand when it is used, should be kept high enough to be seen easily by the entire group. An area almost level with the shoulders and chest seems to be the most effective. The most ineffective position, and the most awkward it seems, is when the hands and arms are kept almost directly down at the sides of the body. Such a position causes most of the hand and arm movements to be hidden from view in which case the meaning of their indications is practically lost to the musicians.

The director should develop a good, definite, distinct and clear beat. One often sees a considerable amount of baton waving and fanning of the air, and sometimes the players and singers do a creditable performance in spite of it. Generally, such exertion is distracting to the audience, and to the musicians especially. The safe course is to be so definite with the beats as to allow no misunderstanding on the part of the players or singers. This, of course, means adhearance to the accepted manner of beating time. To do so avoids confusion when working with strange groups and, too, the musicians will be able to follow other directors better.

The beats should not be pounded out rhythmically perfect for all types and kinds of melodic and harmonic moods. There are times when hand movements need not vary one from the other more than a few inches—perhaps a bare change in hand position will suffice especially when a delicate effect is desired. On the other hand, a very broad, massive and masculine movement may require the full sweep of the arm, and the snappy, brilliant march will require a beat to match. It is not amiss to mention the preparatory beat which so many directors seem to feel is of little importance. The preparatory beat should be in keeping with the type of movement to follow. The march will require a quick, snappy preparatory beat quite in contrast to the preparatory beat of the broader type of movement. The ritard or hold may be indicated not by stopping the stick but by retarding its movement, slowing it to meet the need since the music itself does not stop but is merely delayed.

The cut-off deserves especial attention. Whatever method is used, be sure it is decisive and definite. Some cut off the note or hold with a movement of the stick itself and this seems proper. Others cut off the note with a movement of the left hand. There is some advantage in this since it allows for the continuation of the stick without interruption whereas if the cut-off is made with the stick, it becomes necessary to make a complete new start for the next phrase.

## The Left Hand

There is little use for the left hand in any function where the right hand will suffice yet it should not be left hanging idly beside the body. The left hand might well be kept in front of the body when not in use. This looks much better from the standpoint of the audience, and it is ready for use when necessary without drawing the attention of the audience to the change in position.

Since the primary function of the right hand is to beat the time, the left hand finds itself involved in numerous other details such as indicating to a section, or to a single player, that the entrance is near and then to indicate the exact point of entrance. The left hand is also used to indicate dynamic volume—higher for louder, lower for softer. It may indicate a cut-off, or any one of a dozen things which may come up in the playing of the composition. One thing not necessary is the constant beating of time with the left hand in rhythm with the right hand. Nothing is to be gained by having both hands waving exactly alike and meaning the same thing except when conducting extremely large groups such as a massed chorus, band or orchestra or where such movement of both arms is used to indicate great dynamic power.

The conductor should endeavor to beat the time as clearly as possible, in a manner well understood and in a position easily seen by all concerned. He should endeavor to make all cues such as entrances, exits, dynamics etc., clear and exactly when needed. On the other hand, the player or singer should be so alert as to follow exactly as the conductor indicates. When such is the case, the musician is always right and the director must shoulder any responsibility for success or failure.

The conductor has no way of explaining his desires to the performing group except through the position and motion of his hands and by facial expression. These possibilities should be used to the limit but not to the distraction of the audience.

Lastly, let the actual conducting mean something to the players. Every movement of the baton and the left hand should have a specific meaning. Each bit of vagueness is time lost in the rehearsal. Let it be remembered that wild guestures do not make a group play or sing better, and many a young musician could do a much better job were he not bothered by so many wild gesticulations as is sometimes seen. The surprising thing is that there are remarkable performances in spite of these wild movements. Use discretion at all times. The motions themselves are meaningless unless they represent a method of transmitting the ideas of the conductor to the players. Using the baton is an individual thing. The mechanics of beating three or four to a measure can be taught, but getting results out of the musicians in a rehearsal routine depends on (1) the facial expressions of the director, (2) the expression found in the director's eyes or lips, (3) the fingers and fist of the left hand and (4) the many ways of expressing the mood through the use of the baton itself. These expressions, coming from the innermost musical soul of the director, are the things which can not be taught in the routine of a conducting class. Only patient study of scores, listening to recordings, the hearing of much good music, following the methods of the better conductors and other such study will help the director achieve the success he wants.

Chapter VII

PREPARATION FOR GOOD PRODUCTION

It may well be agreed that the high school musical organization is not made in the high school nor is the college
organization made in college. Of course we have rehearsals
and beginning students in the high school and these have a
lot to do with the success of the school groups but the real
beginning is in the junior high and on down into the grades,
where this is possible. The true musical groundwork should
be laid below the high school level and the success of these
younger organizations is reflected in the success of the high
school and college groups as the young musicians develop
and mature. Such an early start makes three or four years of
musical experience available for every student who reaches
the advanced organizations. If the director expects to develop
his material starting with the freshman year, he will find his
musicians graduating almost before they have learned the fundamentals, and certainly before they are of any great value
to the high school band, orchestra or chorus. The high school
organization is thus deprived of the student's services before
he has had a chance to make use of his training. Start them
young and build well and the performance of the organization will be a source of pride and joy both to the organization
and to the director.

### Groundwork

Of what shall the early preparation consist? The one acceptable groundwork is a thorough understanding and mastery, if possible, of scales, chords, arpeggios, intervals and
groups of scale notes in various rhythm patterns. Whether
this study material comes from some book especially designed
for the purpose or whether suitable passages are taken from
regular pieces used in rehearsal makes little difference. This
groundwork material must come from some source whether
designed or adapted. If it is impossible to have the necessary
supplementary material in the music library, then the director should make an effort to select suitable training material
from the playing material at hand, or write out the necessary
study passages.

Groundwork must include a working knowledge of the fundamentals of music. The student should learn the note values and how long the note should be held according to the various markings. If the note is a dotted quarter note let it be played as such, not as a half note or an eighth. If it is a half note let it receive its full value. Any variation will come later on when the student is in a position to better understand interpretation. The groundwork must be a foundation of right pitches, right note values, correct phrasing procedure, proper attacks and releases. A student well fortified with this foundation is well fortified for more serious additional and advanced study.

### Phrasing

There are three types of phrases: the metrical phrase usually found in groups of four measures; the melodic phrase which expresses a complete thought; and, the rhythmical phrase consisting of notes in sequence which may or may not coincide with the regularity of the metrical beats of the measure. All phrases should receive an accent at the beginning of the phrase on the strength of the importance of its entrance.

All phrases have either a masculine or a feminine ending. The masculine ending is the stronger of the two, ending usually on the first beat of the measure. Sometimes a long note will be the indication of a masculine ending. Both the first beat of a phrase and the long note on which it may end call for a more decisive accent. A masculine ending also obtains when the last note is preceded by a rest or where the phrase ends with syncopation. The phrase is also considered masculine if the last note is re-itterated.

Since all phrases should begin with an accent, let it be remembered that there are three types of accents: first, the dynamic accent; second, the prolonging of a note, and third, preceding the note with a rest. A general rule and a good one to follow is: the shorter the note the softer and lighter it should be sounded; the longer the note, the heavier and more solid it should sound.

Some general rules regarding phrasing may be summed up in the following words:

1. the phrases should hang together from a metrical point of view,

2. in groups of notes, the first note should be accented,

3. a note which finishes a measure, a beat, or a fraction of a beat, if repeated, receives an accent,

4. the longer the note the more it should be accented,

5. a note preceded by a rest should be accented,

6. the quicker the tempo the less the accent,

7. a syncopated note is accented,

8. in rhythmic phrases, the phrase is accented to emphasize the rhythm,

9. when a note changes in pitch in its melodic line, the changed note is accented, that is: if the melodic line is C to C sharp to D, the C sharp would be accented,

10. a prominent change in the harmony (such as a change of key) is accented on its entrance,

11. where a phrase rises to a climax there should be a slight break before the climax,

12. in reaching a dynamic climax, save the height for the climax,

13. a good crescendo effect is made by judicious use of a sudden diminuendo—that is, a sudden let-down emphasizes the height to which the phrase has been lifted,

14. a new phrase entering for the first time or upon its re-appearance should be accented on that entrance, and

15. a phrase of successive notes ascending in pitch should call for a crescendo and, conversely, a group of notes descending in pitch should call for a diminuendo.

## Tonal Balance

An understanding of the fundamentals of good performance is of little value without the opportunity to put them to good use. So, when putting the fundamentals in order, the relative value of one player to another or of one section to another must not be overlooked. It might well be remembered that each beat of every measure contains a solo passage for some instrument or voice set to an accompaniment played or sung by the balance of the organization. Attention to the relationship of solo to accompaniment is insurance against poor tonal balance. One of the most difficult things to teach the young musician is that of playing or singing a fine accompaniment.

While cautioning the bass section about over-playing, a young sousaphonist asked: "Why do we have so many sousaphones yet must play softer? Why not have just one or two sousaphones in the band and then play louder?" The question is a logical one and on the surface seems reasonable. Certainly we do not work for a large clarinet or violin section simply to reach a fortissimo more easily. We do not have large choral sections just to sing loud. The reason for having a great number of vocalists, clarinets, violins, cellos or other instruments in any section is so the resultant tone-color of that section will be richer. Suppose just one clarinet were used and the necessary loudness were achieved through electrical amplification, we would still have just that one tone-color peculiar to that particular player and instrument. Put two players in the section and the tone-color possibilities are increased. Multiply this by the several we strive to have and the result is a color far more beautiful than one instrument alone could give. Such understanding is necessary in striving for tonal balance. When once the young player senses this problem and understands the solution, the director will have little trouble in obtaining cooperation of the student and the section.

Tonal balance, the understanding of which must be a part of the student's preparation, can be attained through much sustained chord work. By using chords in chorale form or chorales themselves much progress will be made. It is possible to attain similar results through using chords selected from the composition in daily use. The chord may be treated in several ways, the initiative of the director is the only limit. One suggested use of chords is to start the tone softly, increasing the dynamics until a fortissimo is reached. While doing this, stress should be laid on an even raise in the level of dynamics by individuals and by sections, making sure that the tone is neither forced nor hardened by the increased intensity. Instrumentally, the less experienced band or orchestra will show a higher level in the brass than in the woodwind. It is thus found that brass plays louder easier than does the woodwind. The balance of the two is one of the director's tonal problems. In teaching and illustrating the facts of tonal balance in dynamic levels, it is possible to also teach the value and need of an even pitch. It is well known that when approaching a fortissimo the brass has a tendency to blow sharp and the clarinets have a tendency to blow flat. Players of these instruments should understand this fact and attempt to overcome it. The reverse is also true. When approaching a pianissimo, the brass has a tendency to blow flat and the clarinets sharp. Thus much attention is required to keep these sections tonally balanced.

The director should avoid the "lip breaker" type of playing and when this seems absolutely necessary, do so only as required and no more. Nothing destroys tonal balance and lip control as does ballyhoo playing. This problem is fronting the director constantly. He finds it necessary to play for all parades, football games, basketball, pep assemblies, track meets and what not and at the same time be able to present a good concert organization. All parties concerned do not seem to realize that the former does not contribute to the latter. Some directors have met this by developing only that kind of a band which serves the school best be it either the ballyhoo band or the concert band. Unfortunately, too many directors have to have both types out of the one mould. The solution is easy for those blessed with numbers for they are able to have at least two organizations: one to do the concert work and one to do the work of the marching and parade band. In other words, an "A" band and a "B" band —each to its own purpose.

Tonal balance will be improved through the encouragement of soft, smooth, round tones. The dull, hard, blattant kind of tone has little place in music. The tone should be as clear as the finest gem, as rich as the finest beverage. When needed, it should be as brilliant and sparkling as the finest champagne but never, never is there a place for the dull, lifeless, inanimate, commonplace tone.

## Detailed Rehearsal

No one will deny the value of attention to details during the rehearsal. There should never be a time when the whole organization plays as if mad; each player for himself and the devil for the last one. Such playing (unfortunately common) shows a decided lack of attention to the details. The director and the listener must be aware at all times of the melody and its accompaniment as well as any counter melodies woven around it. The melody should be clear and definite and the accompaniment subdued to it. This may be helped by having one section sustain a chord while other sections play or sing the arpeggio of the chord thus the arpeggio becomes the solo and the sustained chord is the accompaniment.

The matter of *what* is played must not be overlooked. Too often the director will pride himself on the title of a selection as it appears on his program rather than priding himself on the efficiency with which the number is rendered. Note values should be stressed; the expression marks over exaggerated or at least slightly so—if the part says piano, then play it pianissimo and vice-verse. Also, the greatest amount of practice should be on the hardest parts. In some rehearsals the director will repeat over and over the easy passages often starting at the first of the composition and proceeding to the first difficult spot then returning to the first he will repeat the action instead of carefully segregating the difficult passage and working on it, breaking it into its component parts until the actual trouble is found. A few days of such detective work will pay big dividends in time saved in later rehearsals. Better still, the pupils become imbued with this form of practice and will do it of their own accord when practicing individually.

Of course the director must be conscious of the limitations of his group, working not for symphonic proportions if the voicing or instrumentation and experience does not warrant it. Increasing the size of the group does not necessarily increase its efficieincy and the limit in any case should be that governed by good balance. One way to increase the size of the brass section legitimately is to increase the kinds of brass instruments in the various families. Fluegelhorns may be stressed. There should be no objection to tenor horns especially if used in pairs. Valve trombones are not as objectional as some seem to think——certainly not as objectional as a poorly played bassoon or the ill played saxophone of which we have many and of which we are too often numerically overblessed. Some of these instruments so mis-understood can be of material value in aiding tonal balance. Surely they can be of value in increased participation to say nothing of their increased value in balancing many a chord harmonically thus producing a more complete and well rounded brass section which should contribute toward a better approach to the balance of the whole organization.

Chapter VIII

# REHEARSAL ROUTINE

There are two ways of conducting a rehearsal: (1) the unorganized, ill prepared, hap-hazard, and (2) the rehearsal with a definite aim and purpose. Since the latter type needs only commendation, the former type will be of primary concern. Every director should strive for a smooth sounding, flexible and clean-cut organization yet this objective can not be reached unless the methods of instruction contribute to this goal. The manner in which the director goes about to achieve his goals in rehearsal stamps the directors as efficient or non-efficient.

If the director is really sincere in his work, he will be anxiously looking forward to the time when his organization is able to sight read well with due regard for musical taste. It behooves the director, then, to see that his organization is thoroughly familiar with such requisites as:

1. correct tuning,

2. true intonation,

3. smooth tone,

4. technical ability,

5. tonal balance,

6. dynamics,

7. phrasing, and

8. expression.

The organization with a practical understanding of these qualities, and with experience enough to use them, will easily be placed among the number one organizations of the country be it from the city or from the small town. It must be noted that some of our finest choruses, orchestras and bands, both marching and concert, have come not from the big cities but from the smaller towns.

It has been said that the first duty of the director is to see that the musicians under him understand perfectly what kind of an effect is desired. By achieveing this, the director has saved countless minutes, and probably hours, of precious rehearsal time which would other wise have been lost in a constant repetition of the passage or piece in the vain hope that somewhere along the route the desired interpretation would come about. It behooves the director to give the clearest possible explanation of what he expects of the musicians, a possibility only if the director understands what he wants himself. One sure way of making this possible is a thorough reading of the score and a careful editing of the parts. By editing with the aid of colored pencils, the attention may be called to dynamic markings, bowing, phrasing, changes in tempo or any one of a dozen other indications thought necessary. Some directors have found it quite advantageous to use both a red and a blue pencil, using one color for dynamics only; the other for phrasing, tempo changes etc. A little time spent in this form of editing is multiplied in value in rehearsal time saved.

### Some Reminders

Rules which should be stressed at rehearsals are heard repeatedly—and will bear repeating here. Musical group behavior is an excellent indication of conductorial ability. Every young musician should not only be urged but taught to:

1. Be punctual.

   Oftimes students will look upon the musical groups as something different from regular school routine. Technically, the rehearsal should be a rigid part of the school tardy and absent system. Punctuality saves much rehearsal time; besides, it aids in building the morale in general.

2. Tune quietly and accurately

   This responsibility should lay with the first-chair man. It should be his duty to see that his section is in proper tune—that each one has the proper knowledge of tuning. It is quite necessary that the director have a private session with the first-chair men in this regard. Such procedure will both stimulate and speed the work of the section.

The players should be reminded constantly that the entire rehearsal is a matter of tuning. Accurate intonation can be had only through accurate listening while playing. Also, no matter how accurate the fingering, it is of no value if the instrument is fundamentally out of tune with itself.

3. Hold the instrument correctly

There are two very definite reasons for this: one, the musician will play better and two, he will look better. Correct holding of the instrument makes for better posture generally which, from a physical standpoint, is greatly to be desired. Cornets, trumpets and trombones should be played with bells pointed up not down. French horns should be held so that the mouthpiece and mouth pipe extend straight out from the mouth in a comfortable position—not pointed at an angle toward the floor. The same is true for violins and violas—they should be held up by the pressure of cheek bone on the shoulder and not by the left hand since this hand should be absolutely free to do the fingering of the strings. The director need not be reminded of all the various positions which make for better playing but the players often must be.

4. Have Instrumental accessories

These accessories such as mutes, resin, valve oil, reeds, strings, etc., must of necessity be a part of the instrument. Being without them is like trying to drive a car without sufficient gas.

Other general rules proven valuable by the experience of many directors are:

1. Do not allow individual practice when someone

is on the podium. When the conductor takes his place it is time for practice to stop and the rehearsal to begin.

2. The inside person turns the music and also takes the lower note when there are parts to be divided. This is the general practice among professional organizations and works well with all.

3. The music should be placed in the folder and the folder closed at the end of every rehearsal or concert. It is then ready for the librarian to do with as the director desires.

4. The body should be erect and both feet should be kept squarely on the floor at all times.

All of the above apply equally well to vocal or instrumental, and even those suggestions pertaining directly to the instrumentalists may be adapted to vocal procedure to some extent.

### Processing the Score

The conductor should strive to follow the instrumentation as indicated in the score. Only when the instrumentation at hand makes a change necessary should deviation be made. When substitutions must be made, do so only after much thought and deliberation. It is not wise to make hasty decisions in giving one instrument the complete part of another instrument. Remember, only a flute can sound like a flute or an oboe like an oboe. The director should have great regard for the wishes of the composer and should try as nearly as possible to present that wish of the composer to the listening public.

Of course it is not necessary to study religiously every score which comes to the conductor's stand especially in sight reading, but for concert and other public appearances there should be a close and rigid study of every phrase and every tonal combination. The red and blue pencil should be used generously to mark the score in order that a better picture of the musical structure may be obtained. First, there is the harmonic

balance or the distribution of harmony. Here is an opportunity for the director to make a practical use of his harmony and
counterpoint. Sometimes, where the available instrumentation
is not equal to that called for in the score or where the vocal
sections are unbalanced, a simple re-arrangement of the chord
will make for a better harmonic balance without damage to
the finished product. The most important note in the chord
may appear in a part not present in the ensemble, or it may
appear in what is one of the weaker sections or in a range difficult for the young musician. Such harmonic changes are always permissable where there is an advantage without real
sacrifice.

Second, a similar relationship occurs in working out the
dynamic balance. It may be necessary to chnge the marking
which appears in some parts. The *forte* may need to be changed to *fortissimo*, or the *piano* changed to *pianissimo*. This
may be necessary to preserve a relative balance of parts. Instrumentally, brass plays louder easier (and it is not amiss
to add, more often) than does the woodwind. Vocally, sopranos are often quilty of this over-singing dynamically. If
all four parts of the vocal number, soprano, alto, tenor and
bass, are each marked *forte* and the sopranos, being greater in
number or more powerful in voice, is too outstanding, it will
be necessary to mark the soprano part *piano* in order to compensate the *forte* of the three other parts.

### Melody and Accompaniment

The highest compliment which can be given an organization is praise for it's ability to play or sing a nice accompaniment to solo passages. The conductor, in studying the score,
will do well to separate the melody from the mass of surrounding accompaniment. This is another use for the colored
pencil. The melody may skip from one section to another, or
it may skip from one voice to another within the section.
Where ever the melody may be, the musicians should be
taught to recognize it, playing or singing down below it—
never above. Such artistic accompanying is not limited to
symphonic groups alone, nor to music of symphonic type. It
should be practiced by every playing or singing group in every
number used.

An instrumental illustration may serve well: the melody in the trio of one march is carried mainly by the horns; back of this is a distinct rhythmic accompaniment of bass and trombones. Behind all this is a clarinet background of harmony which may be likened to the canvas on which the pattern is laid. The rhythmic accompaniment is the perspective distance against which the foreground of melodic line is laid. The interpretation should allow all three parts to be heard in that relationship.

## Attacks

The conductor should impress on the musicians the value of various forms of attack. The kind of an attack necessary depends on the type of piece or passage being played or sung, its tempo markings, dynamic markings and its phrasing. Any one or all of these factors may play a controlling part. Common judgement will not allow a player to use the same attack on a ponderous, slow-moving sort of thing that he would use on a light gavotte. A sense of musical judgement can not be taught too early. The conductor should strive for a definite achievement at each rehearsal and attention to attacks is not the least in achievements.

## Expression

The production of music requires much more than a display of technical skill. Technical skill will enable one to sing or play notes in rapid succession and mechanically but never in the world will technical skill alone produce beautiful music. Certain means of expression must be taught just as other fundamentals must be taught. It is natural expression technic to increase the volume as notes go up; to decrease the volume as the notes go down. It is good expression technic to accent the first note of a phrase; to "push out" the larger notes a little more than the smaller notes; to hold the dotted notes to what appears to be slightly longer than is called for; to emphasize chromatically changed notes, and ordinary observation of expression markings will go far toward making a good organization sound much better.

## Intonation

Accurate intonation is of prime importance, there being no value in ensemble music if each individual plays or sings a note of different pitch than that which is written. This is exactly what happens when the group is not playing in tune.

Tuning notes should be sounded in unison and in chords, after first making certain that the instrumentalists have a good understanding of how the tuning note should sound. The term "tuning note" is used with the full realization that no one note can be a permanent tuning guage. By common practice, we generally use the A above middle C on the piano keyboard. There is no reason why C, B, G, or any other note of the chromatic scale should not be used. Is it logical to expect the young instrumentalist to be in time on A and, because of this, be able to play perfectly in tune on every other note of his playing range? Experience shows that this is not the common case. A lack of knowledge of various intervals results in poor intonation. This is equally true among students of the glee clubs and choruses.

Poor intonation can be corrected by studying the intervals, first the octave; then the fifth, adding the third and the sixth in time. These intervals can be combined in many ways to form chords. This is especially of the thirds. Some directors spend a few minutes of every rehearsal in scale and interval study and to remarkable results. Once the director has devised a plan of interval practice, it may be adapted to any and all keys. Interval studies should be used from the time the beginning students can play three notes in a row thus affording a study of the third.

## Tone Quality

Fine group quality can be had only after good individual tone quality has been achieved. Good tone quality should always be glorified and remedies suggested for those poor in tone quality. If at the crossroads as to what constitutes good quality, study some of the better recordings. Even without the aid of recordings, common reasoning would give preference to a rich, velvety, deep resonance over the thin, lifeless tone. The former would certainly be preferred over the coarse, reedy, heavy, noisy quality attained by some. Quite often this latter type of tone results from trying to copy a tone heard via the radio without the student being able to discriminate between a better quality and the poorer quality.

## Tonal Balance

Group tonal balance can not be overstressed. Perfect instrumentation or voicings will not produce it for tonal balance is not produced by numbers alone. In attaining good tonal balance, the tonal volume of single instruments should be modified to suit the necessities of each individual section,, and each section modified to suit the needs of the entire group be it band, orchestra, glee club or chorus.

The best tonal balance is not gained by requiring a certain section to sing or play louder in order to be heard but rather by having the louder playing sections tone down to fit the volume of the weaker sections. If tonal balance is proportioned to the normal singing of the weaker sections rather than having the weak try to sing or play louder, considerable improvement in tonal balance between the individuals and between the sections will be apparent.

## Inspiration

A musical organization will usually do in public just about what is rehearsed in the music room. Sometimes (all too often) organizations have relied on the last minute rehearsal or that bit of last minute inspiration which is sure to come in the final concert or contest. May it be emphasized that it seldom, if ever, arrives. It is well known that the final playing parallels what was learned in the rehearsals. If a final rendition seems to be done miraculously well then there has been some thorough rehearsal procedure somewhere in the past. The organization has achieved a good understanding of the necessary fundamentals pertinent to the good musical performance. Close, diligent study is the making of good performance, and experience will show that perspiration works more wonders than does inspiration.

The director has two jobs. He must look ahead to see what is coming, and he must listen as the music goes by to hear what has just passed. Either of these will require considerable attention yet the double feat is accomplished unknowingly by the director. Through these two un-realized actions the finished product is born. The director is constantly reading ahead of what his ears are hearing and in the process must check, mentally, what the organization is playing or singing with what his eyes have seen, and at the same time he is checking on the music to be played within the next few seconds. By such careful attention the director soon develops a feeling of contact between himself and the musicians which can not be reached by the common practice of just playing pieces. The director is building flexibility.

There is need for some bond between the director and the musicians—some unexplainable connection, workable at the will of the director. Some helps may be necessary to aid the director in attaining this flexibility. One worthy help is that of changing the tempo suddenly or gradually while in rehearsal. The musicians must, of nceessity, learn to keep an eye on the conducting movements of the director. This they soon learn to do as if by a second sight and, too, they develop a sense of musical feeling applicable to the type of number in rehearsal. A second help is the use of much sight reading. Lack of sufficient funds for a large library is often a handicap but the director should make every effort to overcome this and as a last resort he may, possibly, borrow music from neighboring schools for sight reading.

Since the director should be building his music library constantly, he will not overlook the fact that about every three or four years most of his musicians will be sight readers on music purchased before their time. For instance: the music purchased for sight reading this year will be unknown to a greater part of the organization three or four years from now and, too, most players on the second and third parts will have advanced to higher chairs within the same period. Thus, even those who played the piece before are now confronted with an entirely new and strange part for sight reading.

Flexibility is also helped by having the organization play or sing without the director. In addition to giving the musicians the feeling that they must pull together entirely

on their own, the director is able to hear his group from the
same position as the audience. From here he is better able
to correct any effect for tonal balance and general dynamics
as well as general appearance, subjects discussed elsewhere in
this book.

A fourth help in attaining flexibility is to change the seating plan frequently. This is not advised as constant procedure
during the year but an occasional change in seating arrangement is a valuable aid to the players in getting a better understanding of the relationship between their own instrument
and section and others. Of course, this plan should be used
with discretion and with the musicians understanding why.
It is advisable at times to seat the organization in a hodge-
podge manner without regard to any section or family of
instruments—allowing the band and orchestra members to
take any seats they find desirable regardless of instrument. It
is a rare student, indeed, who does not feel some strangeness
in this new seating arrangement but in a hodge-podge arrangement the players will hear new and strange parts they
never knew existed. They will hear the inner parts here and
there, counter melodies, the entrances of strange yet familiar
instruments which until the experiment is tried, they never
heard before. A further advantage in this temporary seating
is that instrumentalists, being fairly well scattered, find it
requires considerable more concentration, attention and alertness on their part.

A fifth help to greater flexibility is through the ensemble
playing, the formation of which is discussed in another
chapter.

There are some common faults which work against the
achievement of a smooth flexibility. Among these is the lack
of attention given to the inner parts. A musical organization
without attention to the inner parts might well be compared
to a pie with no filling. The two crusts are there—the top
or melody, and the bottom or bass—but there is no "goody"
in between to enrich the crusts. The inner parts are indispensable a fact easily demonstrated to the entire satisfaction of the
musicians. Do this by playing a one-finger melody on the
piano, then add a one-finger bass thus showing the bare

skeleton of a composition. Young musicians are quick to catch on. They realize what is lacking. Now play the melody and bass with the addition of the inner parts and see the eyes of the second and third part players light up. They realize their importance. The same illustration may be done with the band by having only the solo cornet and one bass play to illustrate how empty the composition really is when the inner parts are absent. Compare this to the full band with all inner parts. Furthermore, try having the entire band or orchestra play with the exception of those having the melody. It will soon be seen that the melody is only a small part of the total effect and not nearly so important as are many other factors. However, one should not expect great results too soon; that in itself is a common fault and a detriment to good playing. Expecting great results too soon causes a lack of attention to the fundamental rehearsal processes. Often the urge for a *large* band or orchestra contributes to the promoting of students to the advanced group before they are ready for the move. Such promotion generally lessens the ability of the group.

Another fault, and a common one, is the playing of difficult passages at a too rapid pace. Difficult passages should be taken slowly—at the speed which makes it possible for every member to play or sing every note. As soon as each note can be performed mechanically, the speed can be increased gradually until, to the surprise of everyone, the passage is soon performed at the desired tempo. The principal idea is not to lose sight of the rhythmic pattern. If the rhythmic pattern can be understood when a slow tempo is used, there will be little trouble when the tempo is increased.

A final fault is the use of rehearsal time for something other than rehearsal such as stories boastful of the prowess of the director, sarcasm to the musisians, unfunny stories or other such activities remote from the rehearsal of the group. Not much of this will help and too often will decrease the estimation of the director already held by the students. Too often boasting can not be backed up with performance. This brands the director as a prevaricator, and sarcasm brands him as one who has little or no regard for personal feelings. Let the director strive for a full hour of consistent rehearsal with no comments other than those helpful to an increased performing ability.

The rehearsal should move along smoothly with plenty of variety in music, drills and exercises. Should some music prove to be uninteresting to a part of the organization, it should be immediately followed with something of different mood or type. In this way, the rehearsal is seldom dull to the entire organization, and interest is more readily retained.

Lastly, let the rehearsal mean something to the musicians. Every movement of the baton should have a specific meaning; each bit of vagueness is time lost in the rehearsal. The director should make every effort to understand thoroughly the numbers to be used in the rehearsal and should endeavor to make his desires known to the musicians in a clear-cut, definite manner.

Chapter IX

## STYLE AND SHOWMANSHIP

Some directors seem to have a natural flare for style and showmanship; others have style and showmanship in their orgnizations as a reflection of considerable study and effort. In either case, style and showmanship is recognized as an asset to the musical organization and is not to be frowned upon. In fact, a certain amount of it is to be encouraged— not only encouraged but cultivated. The tang of this extra flavor lies in using just the right amount. Too much will spoil the very effect it was intended to create.

### Uniforms

Appearance should be the first consideration and good appearance means a good uniform dress. Some schools spend enormous amounts on brightly colored and highly decorated uniforms. There is always a question to be raised: can the organization match the uniform by its playing or singing? Unless the group can perform as well as the uniform looks there has been created a sort of a hy-bred, a crow with ostrich plumes. This, then, is a financial error. Uniforms cost money; they are the first thing which meets the eye of the audience and they do create an impression, but let us strive to have this fine first impression matched by an equally fine performance. How much better it is to see the organization dressed merely in white shirts, black ties, dark trousers and black shoes and then surpass the uniform by such superior playing that the uniform is forgotten. The organization should have a uniform dress and that completely dominated by a superior musical performance. On the other hand, there are times when uniforms are so elaborate or so brilliant in color as to actually detract from the performance. This is often true among choral groups as well as instrumental.

The use of uniforms designed for a particular purpose or organization is proper. Usually there is a conflict of opinions in regard to the style and color when new uniforms are purchased. For band, some still believe faithfully in the *cape* type; others adhere strictly to the *coat*. Both have their advantages with the latter in the lead whether it be the military style coat or the close fitting West Point. If, for financial reasons, the coat is out of the question then by all means purchase the cape which is cheaper. It has another advantage, being much easier to pass on from one youngster to another without alteration. This is seldom true with the coat. For this reason it is much wiser to have a few more coat style uniforms than there are members in the band. To do so will save considerable alterations and will keep the uniforms looking better generally saving the cost of extra uniforms in the long run.

## Financing Uniforms

Some schools furnish the entire uniform. Other schools expect the student to buy the complete outfit. This depends on the financial status of the school or the community. Where possible it seems most satisfactory if the school owns the uniforms since they are used over and over again regardless of the changes in personnel.

Some schools have found it quite convenient and satisfactory to work out a three year plan. By this plan, the caps are bought the first year; the trousers the second year, and the coats are purchased the third year. This plan lessens the financial burden and does have some psychological value in that there is a continual uniform interest. There are drawbacks, however, in that at no time does the band ever have a completely *new* uniform. Furthermore, there is always the possibility of failure to match the quality, texture and color of the cloth.

Another plan found successful by some schools allows for the purchase of the caps and coats by the school, the trousers to be purchased by the individual with the understanding that the school may buy the trousers whenever the student graduates or leaves the school. A depreciation scale is set up causing only a small loss to the original purchaser considering his use of the trousers. In one school the trousers cost $11.00 each and depreciation was set at $2.00 per year. Thus, a band member graduating after using his uniform for two years would sell the trousers to the school for seven dollars. In a short time the entire uniform becomes the property of the school and the burden of purchase has not been too great on any party concerned.

## Used Uniforms

Used band uniforms like any other material is difficult to sell for what the seller knows it to be worth and difficult to buy for what the buyer thinks it is worth. If a band is in dire need of uniforms and new ones can not be had, there is no reason why used uniforms in excellent condition should not be used. Many bands are eager to sell their uniforms as part of their money raising campaign for new ones. In buying used uniforms, certain color desires may have to be sacrificed as may also preferred styles. Certainly the quality of material and its condition are of more importance than color and style. While a combination of quality, condition, color and style would be ideal, it is quite possible that one or more of these factors may have to be sacrificed.

If contact has been made in regard to buying used uniforms, it is better to make a trip to look over the lot than to have a sample uniform sent providing the schools are not too far apart. It may be possible that some acquaintance in the area of the seller may be called upon to inspect the uniforms, and it may be that the seller will ship the entire lot C.O.D., subject to inspection. In all events, it is better to purchase more uniforms than is needed so that only the best will be chosen for immediate use.

## Buying New Uniforms

Whatever the uniform may be, purchase only from a thoroughly reliable company—one which will give exactly what is wanted and what is promised. If there is any doubt about a maker, feel free to write any neighboring band man concerning his experience with this or any other company. The band director is usually in a better position to know this than the school administrator.

The material and workmanship should be of the very best the budget will allow as should also the quality of cloth. Generally, color does not alter the price since most qualities come in the same colors. In the past, schools have been quite consistent in retaining the school colors when choosing band uniforms. In recent years, it is becoming more and more noticable that schools are choosing colors for the benefit of the organization rather than to show the colors of the school. This is entirely practical for many colors which look good as a pennant are certainly unbecoming in the form of a uniform. One shool which has colors of purple and gold bought their first band uniforms in red and white because of the better show this color makes on the night playing field. The second outfit bought by this school was of the two-color blue—dark blue coat and light blue trousers—reasoning that this uniform would both look good on the marching field and serve well as a concert uniform. Another school has colors of red and white but bought band uniforms of navy blue with gold trim counting on this as being more practical and servicable.

It is not advisable to have uniforms made up in school colors if the school colors are out of the ordinary in shade, or if the color is unusual. Odd shades and unusual colors often create a problem of matching color when new uniforms are added in the future, and sometimes mean the buying of a complete new outfit before it is needed because the original color can not be matched. One school, over a period of years, ended up with band uniforms of three shades of green to say nothing of the off-shades caused by fading.

Sometimes uniforms are bought by dealing with a single company especially where the company has furnished the uniforms in the past. The school simply states its desires and the company states a price usually with possible optional changes and a corresponding price change. Sometimes the uniform company makes up the uniform design and sets a price on it, the school accepting and agreeing to it. Others encourage keen bidding, looking primarily to the quoted price. There is danger in this unless the purchaser knows the uniform business as well as does the manufacturer. Low bids sometimes eliminate small items which must be purchased later much to the sorrow of the school—and oftimes to a higher total uniform cost. If bidding is desired, be certain that everything is included in the bid price since everything not included must be purchased at regular retail price. Always insist on having prices quoted clearly on every item you in-

tend to buy. Business is business and no friendly relatiofiship
with the dealer or salesman will substitute for it. Besides, if
the dealer or salesman is really a friend he will make every
effort to see that you get a square deal and will gladly cooperate by setting all matters in black and white.

## Attention and Posture

Alertness and attention are a necessary part of a good performance and also are a part of good showmanship not only
creating the impression of interest but being an actual aid to
better performance. Good posture must be added to alertness
and attention. Nothing shows faulty training quicker than
does poor posture. Correct posture does not stop with simply
sitting up straight in the chair, nor simply remaining upright. Instrumentally, cornets, trumpets and trombones not
only play better but look decidedly better when held *up*
rather than with bells pointing to the floor. A good looking
position and a comfortable one will allow the director to
look almost directly into the bells from his position on the
podium. Many of our young trumpet and trombone players
have taken a mis-cue from some jazz players and have gone
to the extreme in the manner of holding instruments. In
many cases they not only look ridiculous but have decreased
their playing ability.

## Holding the Instrument

Before playing and between numbers, the players should
be unified in the manner of holding instruments. It is not
good style nor good showmanship to have part of the players holding instruments up, part of them laying the instruments down, some perhaps leaning on the instrument. Whatever may be decided upon, let it be of a uniform nature, not
hit and miss. This should always be a part of the regular
rehearsal training of the organization. Holding the instruments nicely should not be the result of last minute warnings. These last minute warnings are plainly noticeable and
easy to detect for some players will have the instrument correctly placed as advised; some never will, and a few will
start leaning on the instrument then suddenly realize the
instrument should be held in a certain position and immediately place it in that position only to accompany the

movement by a sheepish grin and crossed legs. Then he discovers his legs are crossed and so uncrosses them with another embarrassed grin only to be nudged by his neighbor and reminded to get the instrument up in position—only to realize that he has "scooted down" in his chair. By the time he has corrected this he finds the band well started into the next number; he hastily starts playing and suddenly discovers he is patting his foot—it goes on and on, noticeable to everyone in the audience—and the illustration is not overdrawn.

## The Percussion

Nothing seems to thrill the audience as does a perfectly smooth working drum section. With perfect timing of beats, perfect raising and lowering of sticks, perfect syncronization in being at the proper instrument at the proper time, graceful handling of the bass drum stick, nice flashy cymbal work, no section can out-show the percussion section providing such is not overdone. Herein, of course, lies the secret of all showmanship—the art of knowing when to stop being good.

With all the above, no section receives less attention than does the drums yet it should receive the most. A good drum section can MAKE the band; a poor section can ruin it. Each individual member of the drum section should develop a certain amount of style. The snare drummers should develop good, smooth, even "sticking" but should avoid the extreme fancy twirling more appropriate to the majorettes. The style and showmanship coming from the drum section should reflect good rudimental playing with appropriate arm movements but *never* with wild, baton-twirling stunts. The same should be true of the bass drummer. Occasionally one sees such swinging of the bass drum stick in the air and so little of it musically on the drum that the section would be greatly improved by a change in drummers. Similar cautions should be made to the cymbal player. It should be remembered that a better tone as well as a better appearance can be had if the cymbals are held and struck about shoulder high. Cymbals should be struck by moving each in the opposite direction in an arc, the blow being a glancing one as the cymbals come together in the center of the two opposing arcs. The cymbal tone should not be stopped by a directly horizontal blow but by bringing them against the body immediately after striking.

It must be remembered that in most of our school bands and orchestras the percussion section stands, a position which makes it possible for the audience to see the section at all times. This added height actually calls attention to the section so, while the section should be keen and alert at all times as well as at attention, the faces should have a pleasant look. Try to avoid the hard, "dead-pan" effect so often seen. Become alive and alert!

### Brass Instruments

A fine brass section should be given the same opportunity as is afforded the percussion section. This applies primarily to the cornets, trumpets and trombones. Due to their shape these instruments lend themselves to showmanship better than do those instruments manufactured in coils. The posture should require the use of the entire seat of the chair not just the front edge. The body should be upright and straight but not stiff. Arms should be free of the body and not using it as a support. While these sections are seated and the playing level lower, it is easy to see the slouchy player. This attitude toward good posture is not beneficial to the band or orchestra and does not add to the general effect of the section. Bells should be up, slides high and military precision all combine to give the audience the feeling that the entire section knows what it is all about and that they are really giving something to the organization.

### Strings

The above applies equally well to the string sections even more so since they are the foundation of the orchestra. The violins being toward the audience, as are sometimes the violas or cellos, receive the major attention of the audience which usually sees before it hears. Violins should be held with the violin neck pointing up rather than down, and bowing should be uniform.

### Attitude

The director has a right to expect, and certainly should

seek, a responsive and alert attitude on the part of the student musicians. At no time should the attitude be one of stiffness and artificiality, certainly not to the point of handicapping the organization. There must be some relaxation, in fact there should be perfect relaxation. At all times, students should feel free to ask questions or discuss musical questions with the director and he should encourage it. The director ought, also, to be able to draw the line between his position as teacher and that of the musician as a student. Any familiarity with the students should be that which encourages respect and appreciation rather than that which breeds contempt.

### Choral Groups

Choral groups should stand erect, with heads up and eyes bright. The arms should be held in a uniform manner whether in front or back of the body. The weight of the body should be supported by both feet equally. If the music is not memorized, the music should be kept in the folders to prevent any detraction due to the handling or turning of the many white pages of music paper.

The choral groups should use risers with the shorter singers on the front row. Not only will the chorus be better able to see the director but the tones will carry through much better. As with instrumental groups, the use of a uniform dress will greatly enhance the appearance of the organization, and the use of robes in a well chosen color and style will be of far greater value than the original cost might indicate.

### The Director

Finally, a word of caution to the director about his part of style and showmanship. The American audience enjoys showmanship and to some extent expects it from the conductor. Although this is a wrong conception of the duties of the conductor, some try to include it among their duties on the podium. Showmanship in small quantities is excellent but it should never be overdone. Too often the line of demarcation is unknown. The director will do well to see that he is dressed correctly for the occasion, that he is free from tense-

ness and rigidity when conducting. The tenseness experienced by the director and exhibited before his students is too
often reflected in their performance. Confidence should be
instilled in the players or singers—even a little cockyness,
if necessary. A smile from the director just before performing the number is worth a thousand tense, hard-boiled looks.
Let the director be the one who sets the psychological pace
for the musicians through his actions, words and appearance.

Chapter X

SEATING ARRANGEMENTS

There seems to be as many possible seating arrangements as there are thoughts on the subject and any one of them may be a most satisfactory seating for some particular organization. An open mind on seating arrangement is not only a healthy condition but one which points to good experimentation toward a specific purpose. Some experimentation in the seating plan of the chorus, orchestra or band will result in an arrangement approaching perfection for the organization regardless of its voicings. What is right and what is wrong in seating arrangements amounts to this: any seating arrangement is right when it affords the best possible results with the ability at hand.

There are many factors which enter into the problem of proper seating. Above all, the director should not allow prejudice to enter into his choice of seating; neither should he follow explicitly the seating arrangement of some other groups unless he has experimented with the arrangement and found it satisfactory to his own type of organization. Some of the important factors which affect the seating arrangement are:

1. The tone quality of the various sections

It may be safely assumed that no director has ever had an organization which had perfect tonal quality as a whole, or, for that matter, perfect tone quality in each of its various sections. This is true of the finest professional organizations as well as of non-professional for as the sections improve in tone quality so does the ideal of perfection improve. This will be found even more true for the amateur school group.

It is the audience which receives the final effect of the musical qualities of the group. For that reason, it is advantageous to experiment with the placing of the various sections and even the seating of the members within the sections. Some find it advantageous to place the inferior musicians toward the center of the section with the superior musicians on the outside, claiming this procedure gives the section a more solid body of tone by allowing as little as possible of the inferior, weaker tones to come through. This may be extended to the whole organization, placing the strong sections on the outside and the weaker ones near the center. In other words, surround the inferior with the superior and thus fortify the better tone quality as much as that can be done.

Some directors place the superior sections nearer the front where this is possible. What this amounts to is a sort of a musical filter. Of course it is not possible to suggest substitutes for an organization with poor tone quality. The nearest known short-cut is that of long and tedious musical drill.

2. Need of accurate rhythm.

The necessity for accurate rhythm, and the ability of the group to sense it, should be a factor in any seating arrangement. This applies particularly to the instrumentalists and especially to the rhythm sections of band and orchestras—the drums, basses and the horns.

Some directors find it advantageous when planning the seating arrangement to place a good musician along side of a poor musician and thus even up the entire section. This has advantages in that each good musician becomes a teacher of the poorer musician; he becomes a supervisor, advisor and guide. Many directors attest that this manner of seating will materially improve the rhythm and phrasing of a section due to the experience of the older members.

The location of the drums is highly important. While other sections such as basses and horns are rhythmic as well as harmonic, the one sole purpose of the drums is rhythmic. The location of the drums will have much to do with the entire rhythm of the organization and placing them in the center-back will have a stabilizing effect throughout the group. If the bass drummer is unusually good, place him as near the back center of the band as is possible. This means the bass drummer will be on the left of the precussion section if the section is to the director's left or on the right if the section is on the director's right. Centering the bass drum aids materially in obtaining a steady rhythm.

A similar reasoning should be followed with the basses, keeping them as near their related sections as is possible. Some directors have found it possible to divide the bass section when the section is of sufficient quality to warrant a division without loss of character or without any problems in keeping a steady rhythm. When the bass section is divided, the percussion is usually placed between the two bass sections. This helps tie the rhythm together as one section.

3. Seating by instrumental families.

The seating of instrumental families has always been a problem with band men, the usual procedure has been to imitate the seating of the orchestra. This is a false procedure. The band is an organization complete within itself just as the orchestra is, except that it is more limited in tonal color possibilities than is the orchestra which contains all the instruments of the band and in addition the four groups in the string family. To obtain the best possible results from the instrumentation at hand requires considerable thought on the proper placing of each section and each individual within the section.

Using the orchestra as a pattern, the clarinet section has been divided as the customary manner of dividing the violins, placing the first clarinets on the left and the second clarinets on the right. Band dirtctors (as well as orchestra directors) have seen the error of this division in that it divides the body of tone color and seems no more reasonable than does the division of the trombones or horns or flutes. A director would not tolerate the suggestion that he place his first trombonists on the left and his second and third trombonists on the right, or doing the same with the first and second horns.

The greatest of instruments, the pipe organ, is a splendid example to follow in building up a balance of band or orchestral tone colors. The pipe organ is built on the premise that like families of stops (instruments) should be grouped together. They are grouped together as solo voices, orchestral voices as dynamic groups, that is: like tone colors or like kind.

The net advice is to keep the rhythm together as nearly as is possible, group all sections according to tone colors and according to the part they play or reinforce, and try to keep those instruments of like kind near each other.

4. Showmanship

The term showmanship is not always a popular one but it can not be ignored even in our seating arrangements. A fine cello section should be placed where it can be seen as well as heard; so should a fine flute section or any other section so long as its placement does not hinder the tonal balance of the band or orchestra. The director need not be ashamed of showmanship in this case if he has something to show.

### Instrumental Seating Arrangements

The following seating arrangements are actual plans used by fine bands and orchestras many of which are state and national winning organizations as well as college and university bands. The plans are presented only as suggestions, hoping they will serve as a stimulant; that they may be of some aid to the director in his experimentation.

### The Band

Seating Plan No. 1 is a conventional seating arrangement, having been found advantageous from many angles especially in its flexibility since this plan may easily be altered to meet the instrumentation and size of most any band.

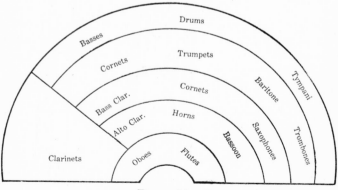

PLAN NO. I

Seating arrangements No. II and III have some advantage over the more conventional Plan No. I in that this manner of seating allows almost every member of the band to have a better view of the director who is able to face directly each member of the organization. No section is slighted in attention even when the director is concerned with only one part of the group since there needs be no turning from one side to the other during the conducting. In the conventional seating arrangement (No. I), the players on the left are somewhat at a loss when the director turns to those on his right. In addition, some directors claim this manner of seating (Plans No. II and III) creates a more compact band and a better tonal effect.

The number of rows used and the exact manner of seating the sections is a matter of judgment on the part of the director. Where a seating arrangement of straight rows is used (such as Plan No. II), the players should be seated at a slight angle in order to face the director. Those on the director's right should face slightly toward the director's left (the player's right) and those players sitting on the left should face slightly to the opposite direction. The players in the center sections will face straight forward.

| Drums | Tympani | | Basses | Baritone | Trombones |
|---|---|---|---|---|---|
| Cornets | Trumpets | Bassoon | Bass Clar. | Alto Clar. | Saxophones |
| 4th Clarinets | | Oboes | | Horns | 3rd Clarinets |
| 1st Clarinets | | | Flutes | | 2nd Clarinets |

PLAN NO. II

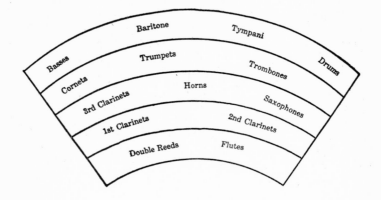

PLAN No. III

Seating Plan No. IV has the disadvantage of dividing the clarinet tone. This older plan is rapidly being replaced by plans which make the clarinet tone more compact and effective, yet there are those who still feel this seating plan is proper for their use. As mentioned before, this plan is an imitation of the conventional orchestral seating arrangement in which the violins are divided. In the band plan, the clarinets are treated as are the violins in the orchestra. If this plan is valuable, perhaps it might be wise to divide all sections, putting the firsts on the left and the seconds and thirds on the right. Such an extreme proposition shows the ineffectiveness of such seating.

Plans V and VI parallell the old military band seating arrangement and is used by many directors with success, especially with the smaller bands. The disadvantage for a large band lies in that strong cornet-trumpet tone is directly in front. In a small band this placement is of little consequence, and does fill out the form of the band since there is usually a shortage of double reeds and flutes, instruments often placed on the right where the cornets are in Plan V and VI.

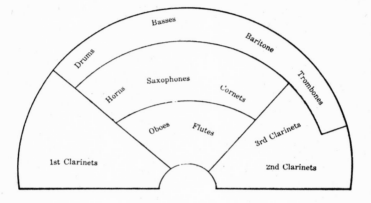

PLAN NO. IV

Plan VII is similar to plan IV but offers a more compact arrangement of the brass, double reeds, low single reeds and the saxaphones.

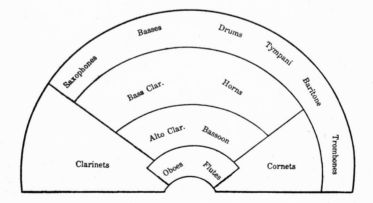

PLAN NO. V

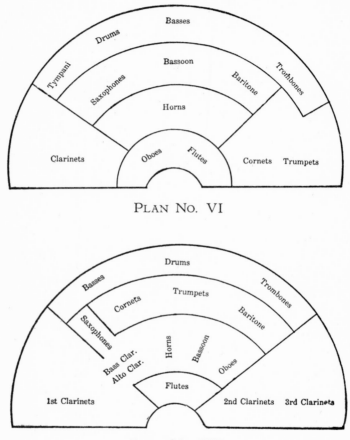

PLAN No. VI

PLAN No. VII

Seating arrangement No. VIII is some departure from the other plans but has the advantage of centralizing the wood-wind tone in one body thus giving a solidness and firmness not obtained otherwise. Pianissimos are obtained easier and there is a unity in the brass due to the placing of the trombones, baritones and basses and the saxophones so that they form a very compact group back of the woodwind.

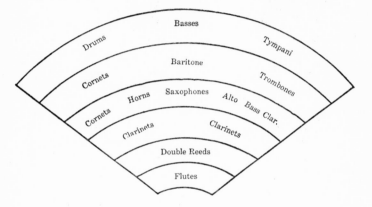

PLAN NO. VIII

*Accoustical Families*

The relationship of the instrumental families should always be borne in mind when planning a seating arrangement. Keep in mind that there are two accoustical families within the brass and woodwind. These are conical and cylindrical. In the conical there are:

Cornet
Fluegelhorn
Melophone
Baritone
Tuba
Sousaphone
French Horn

The brass cylindrical includes:

Trumpet
Tenor trombone
Bass trombone

The French horn may, by some stretch of the imagination, be listed under both classifications since the amount of cylindrical tubing is quite surprising when calculated, being approximately three fourths of its entire length. In placing the brass sections, it would be wise to keep conical with conical and cylindrical with cylindrical, in so far as this is possible.

The woodwind consists of both conical and cylindrical instruments with the added complication of single reeds, double reeds and no reeds at all. In the conical family there are the:

> Oboe
> English horn
> Bassoon
> Contra Bassoon
> Saxophones

In the cylindrical family:

> Soprano clarinet
> Alto clarinet
> Bass clarinet
> Flute

In addition to the type of body used in the manufacture of woodwind instruments, there are:

| *Single reed conical* | *Double reed conical* |
|---|---|
| Saxophones | Oboe |
| | Bassoon |
| | Contra bassoon |
| | English horn |

| *Single reed cylindrical* | *Cylindrical—no reed* |
|---|---|
| Clarinets | Piccolo |
| | Flute |

From this analysis, it is quite apparent that personal notions as to seating may not be the best for the group to be seated, and should one arrangement prove successful this year it may be a disadvantage next year. The changing size of sections in the school band plus a constant changing of the individuals as they grow and develop through the years require the experimentation in seating plans.

## The Orchestra

The same reasoning applied to the band is also applicable to orchestral seating arrangements. Experience shows the wisdom of keeping together those instruments of like voicing, especially those within their own kind. It is not necessary to divide the violins, firsts from the seconds, any more than it is necessary to separate the violas, cellos or basses on a divided part.

Of the suggested seating arrangements, it is obvious that seating plans I and II would be less effective than the remaining plans. A compact section of violin tone as pictured in plan III or IV is ideal, leaving the violas or cellos to be placed at the right. The viola tone may best be heard if they are placed on the right but the cellos, especially if they are abundant in technique, tone and appearance, may well deserve such a prominent place. It is apparent that the high school and college orchestra may easily have a good cello section long before it has an equally good viola section. The general feeling is that the string tone reaches the audience best if the f holes can be placed toward the audience.

It remains here, as in band, for the director to experiment through listening at some distance and from various parts of the auditorium, using various changes in seating arrangements while playing the same number.

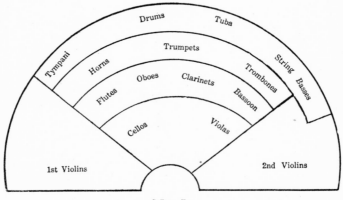

No. I

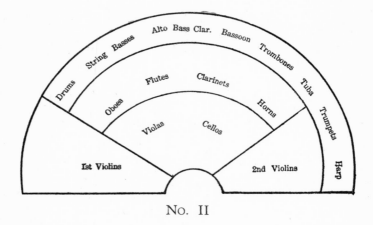

No. II

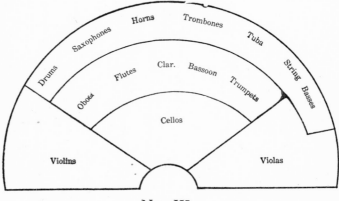

No. III

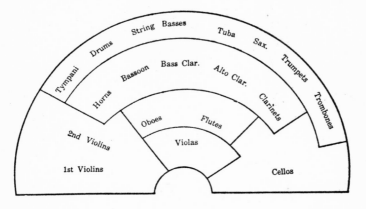

No. IV

Ideas on proper seating arrangements can not become static. The up-and-coming music director will not permit this to happen. If the conductors of our professional symphony orchestras are concerned over the most advantageous seating arrangement, it certainly behooves the school music director to follow suit. Some of our leading symphony conductors have devised and used some rather striking seating plans and at least one has experimented with a plan approximately like the following:

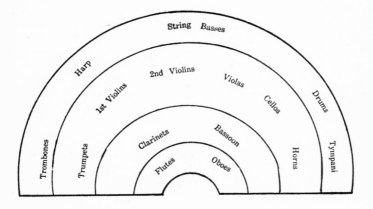

## Choral Seating

The choral director has fewer difficulties in seating arrangements due to a smaller number of group classifications, usually four sections suffice in either mixed chorus or men's glee club; SATB in the former and TTBB in the latter. In other groups the sections may be either two or three, SA, SSA or SAB. This is considerably simpler than the complex situation of band and orchestra where the director must work with twelve or fifteen kinds of voice-sections and many of those divided in parts.

Yet, with its apparent simplicity, the seating of a vocal group requires some study and some changing as the body of tone varies from time to time. The place of rehearsal, places of performance, kind of voices and the type of music all have much to do with the seating plan. The singers may be seated in the conventional manner with little or no thought given to possible improvement but arrangements successful with some voices may be less so with others. Choral seating has no rule except the results obtained, and many directors believe thoroughly in trying various seating plans, changing constantly throughout the year.

## The Chorus

| Bass | Tenor |
|---------|-------|
| Soprano | Alto |

### PLAN NO. I

The conventionally accepted arrangement is Plan No. I, a plan which keeps the tenors and the altos together since their parts oftimes parallel, and the bass and soprano being so placed will sing better in tune.

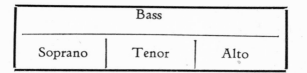

PLAN NO. II

Plan No. II shows an excellent arrangement if the tenor section is weak since it brings them to the front, a position which does not hinder the tone from reaching the audience directly.

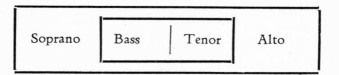

PLAN NO. III

Plan No. III has the basses and tenors surrounded by the sopranos and altos, valuable where unusually strong male voices may be tempered by the feminine or where the sopranos and altos are not strong and must be brought to the front. It may also serve well where the altos are needed to strengthen the tenor part.

Any seating arrangement should be one in which further division of voices may be made with as little defect as possible.

Another suggestion, and one toyed with occasionally, is that of dividing the choral group into several sections known merely by numbers or letters. These sections are selected according to voice quality and range with the former taking precedence. By so doing, a greater variety of tone color is available for choral effects. For instance, if a director finds he can effectively divide his organization into several groups

each composed of nearly identical voices he will then designate which group shall or shall not sing at certain points in
the music. The usual four-part voicing gives way to a
wider conception of tonal color and tone-color blending.

Finally, the most effective appearance both in sight and
sound will be through the use of risers. The advantage is
two-fold: first, the director can see the whole chorus and
every member can see the director and second, every voice is
free to flow directly out to the audience. Risers may be
purchased at a very reasonable cost and the advantages outweigh the cost by far. Sections usually accommodate about
fifteen singers in four tiers, the first row standing on the
floor. While the choir or chorus may sing well seated, the
general appearance is considerably better when standing.
This is especially true when each row of singers is raised
slightly above the row in front.

The advantages of a sub-divided section are easily apparent in that the possibilities of part singing are increased
according to the number of sub-divisions. Plan No. IV illustrates such sub-divison:

| | |
|---|---|
| Baritone | 2nd. Tenor |
| 2nd. Bass | 1st. Tenor |
| 1st. Soprano | 1st. Alto |
| 2nd. Soprano | 2nd. Alto |

Here the strength lies in a choir of the stronger voices within the large group. A complete choir of second bass, first
tenor, soprano and alto lies within the chorus.

Some directors prefer to alternate strong and weak members of each section as:

| | |
|---|---|
| BbB bBbBbBb | TtTtTtTtTt |
| SsSsSsSsSs | AaAaAaAaAa |

Such an arrangement has the advantage in that the stronger singers are a help to the weaker ones, helping them in reading both pitch and rhythm. To alternate singers according to voice quality and range would have a detrimental effect rather than being an aid. Such an arrangement as the following is not recommended:

| BTBTBTBTBTBTBTBT |
| SASASASASASASASA |

Such an arrangement may cause the singers who are weak in reading to sing whatever the one next to them sings. Thus, a weak alto will probably follow a strong soprano and vice versa.

### Glee Clubs

In glee clubs, the same reasoning applies as in the choir or chorus. For boys, the following or its reverse is a common arrangement:

| 2nd. Bass | Baritone |
| 1st. Tenor | 2nd. Tenor |

For girls it might be:

| 2nd. Soprano | 1st. Alto |
| 1st. Soprano | 2nd. Alto |

A more common arrangement might have the first sopranos and first altos in front with the second sopranos and second altos in the rear. The advantage of having the first altos in

the rear is that they might join with the second sopranos
for three part work with greater unity of tone than if part
of the front row had to sing with part of the back row.
Again, the front row of second sopranos and first altos
might join with the first sopranos when necessary. Thus,
this one arrangement may well serve any variety of two, three
or four part singing.

Chapter XI

# THE TWELVE-YEAR PROGRAM

Fortunate indeed is the director who is not content with junior and senior high school band alone but who feels that music in the public school means exactly that; running the gamut through grades one to twelve. A common complaint is that the school is too small to support a wide-range program. This need not be true since musical achievement is not measured by numbers alone. There is no great achievement where a city school of one thousand students has a band, an orchestra or a chorus of only fifty members. Many schools one-tenth this large will have a musical organization of that size. The music director should build the music program in terms of the percentage of students active in music. The school of one-thousand students has a small percentage of students in music, indeed, if only fifty are participating— the amount being five per cent. The school with an enrollment of one hundred has a percentage of fifty if they have fifty students participating in music. Many directors feel that ten per cent is a very low percentage of students to have in music organizations. Fifty per cent seems high. Other directors feel that at the very lowest they should have twenty-five per cent of the junior and senior high school students active in music.

## The Lower Grades

The logical way to build this percentage is to increase the music activity and interest in the lower grades—a field too often accepted but seldom acted upon. No greater opportunity exists for the teaching of music than in the elementary grades and few fields, if any, offer greater opportunities for enthusiasm and ingenuity. Exploring the lower grades for musical talent is to be commended, and the music director will lose no time in encouraging and assisting the lower grade teachers in building rhythm bands and other activities connected with the music program.

The rhythm band affords an excellent outlet for musical aptitude and it can be adapted to the musical level of all players. This can be done by carefully editing the scores bought or, better still, by writing out various rhythm parts for the various instruments. In this way, the more difficult parts may be written for the students of rapid advancement, and the simpler parts for the slower students. The latter may of necessity be a part in which the player plays only on each beat while the former may include intricate rhythmic patterns for advanced students. This possibility of adaptation to the rhythmic level of any student is one of the greatest assets of the rhythm band.

### Flute Bands

As the students advance in their understanding of some of the more common and basic rhythm patterns, it becomes necessary to advance them in their playing level. This can be done through the use of some kind of a flute-like instrument. There are several instruments of this type on the market and excellent results have come from their use. These flute-like instruments are inexpensive, easy to play and simple in operation. Most of them are made with a movable mouthpiece thus having the advantage of a tuning range. Just what this advantage may be to elementary students is debatable. These instruments are built in the key of C and may be played along with the piano, violin or other instruments pitched in the key of C. They may be played in solo, duet or trio form thus opening considerable latitude in playing performance. Even in these early flute classes (usually the third and fourth grades), there is the possibility of small ensembles, those selected from the class as a whole. The limit in what they should play and in how many parts is bounded only by the ingenuity of the director.

### The Value of this Training

It is almost necessary to have some connecting link between the rhythm band and the more advanced stage of orchestral instruments. The flute-like instrument fills this need. Their use encourages and holds musical interest during this early period. In addition, these instruments serve in several other capacities as well. These pre-band and pre-orchestra groups are *talent finders*. It is during this stage that the director begins to find the individuals who have a natural leaning toward music. This period also develops *ensemble thinking*. There is also the development of *independence* and *individuality* as opposed to the first two grades in rhythm band work where all activity is the direct result of suggestion by the teacher. Ensemble playing and ensemble thinking are greatly to be desired as a part of the junior and senior high school music program, vocal or instrumental, and its beginning may be found in these early flute classes.

Since the music is primarily melodic, the young students learn to think in a melodic line and the training through this melodic line is extended when ensemble playing is encouraged. In addition, ensemble playing, other than in unison, is the beginning of the development of harmonic thinking—the realization of *vertical* music as well as *horizontal* music. Here, then, is the first opportunity for training in good intonation. Finally, there is opportunity here for the beginning of sight reading—a development which will pay dividends later in the high school organizations. These factors are equally valuable to the vocal student as well as the instrumental, and the wise vocal music director will encourage instrumental reading in these pre-band classes. Most vocal music teachers will readily admit the advanced sight-reading abilities of the instrumentally trained student over the student who has not had this advantage.

## The Carry-over

The amount of carry-over from the "flute" period into the more advanced music groups is quite evident. A certain amount of this early training is of definite carry-over regardless of the field of music, vocal or instrumental, in which the student enters later. Rhythm, phrasing, note reading, key signatures and clefs are carry-overs common to both fields. For the instrumental student, there is even more carry-over especially for those students who become players of the flute , oboe, clarinet, bassoon and saxophone since the fingering system of these instruments is based on three holes for the first three fingers of each hand, a system basic with the flute-like training instrument. While the actual fingered notes can not be the same for all these woodwind instruments, the principle is the same and in this lies the carry-over.

Another carry-over is the method of tonguing. Correct methods of tonguing should be taught on these pre-band instruments not waiting until the student has passed this stage to find out there is such a thing as a tonguing method. The common fault in producing tones on these flute-like instruments is that they are usually just blown. The teacher of the flute band should know the advantages of a well tongued tone and understand how to produce this better tone. Poor intonation is the result of poor tonguing as is also faulty attacks and releases.

There is a further carry-over for both vocal and instrumental students if the use of the F clef is introduced during this training period. There is no reason why young musicians should not be taught to use the bass clef as well as the G or treble clef. Their future musical life is closely related to both clefs. There should be no problems in teaching the reading of either clef since one is merely an extension of the other. However the use of the F or bass clef will necessitate the re-writing of several parts as its use is not common at this early stage of training.

### Beginning Band and Orchestra

Advancement from the flute-band to the typical band and orchestral instruments seldom takes place before the student has reached the fourth grade. Many directors prefer not to accept band and orchestral students below the fifth grade—this seems a satisfactory year in which to make the change. While the students are not yet ready for a definite assignment to a definite instrument, they are ready for advancement to a true band or orchestral instrument of some kind. The director should not make a definite committment until he is thoroughly convinced that instrument and pupil fit each other perfectly.

Generally, the students are ready to be assigned the violin, flute, clarinet, cornet, piano or percussion but are still to be considered in the pre-training period. Many students may need to be shifted from one instrument to another as they develop physically and mentally.

Small ensembles should be organized and encouraged at all levels, the only difference being that the student has changed instruments but otherwise experiences no change in the procedure. He should continue in ensemble playing, thinking in terms of the widened scope of musical possibilities. This is the period of further development for those young students who show possibilities yet lack some fundamental training. For the others, it becomes a period of beginning instrumental mechanics—the beginning of technical training. However, the director should still consider this not so much as a period for teaching the *instrument* as it is a period for teaching *music* through the use of the instrument. It must be remembered that the student in instrumental music is also continuing his regular music studies in the grade school music program.

## The Junior High School

As the student comes nearer his junior high years he also comes nearer the instrument which is to be his throughout the remainder of his school music life; perhaps to the end of his days. The violin players may find it necessary to take up viola, cello or string bass; the clarinet players may become performers on the bass or alto clarinet, the oboe or bassoon. Some of the cornet players will make good baritone, trombone, bass horn or French horn players and the pianists may develop into players of tympani or other percussion, or may turn to one of the other above mentioned instruments. This decision lies largely with the music director and is one requiring serious thought. Too often the decisions are tempered by the immediate need for certain instruments in the organization. This should not be the only guage and certainly it is not the true one.

During this period ,the young students are undergoing not only an evolution in musical prowess but are entering a perioid of physical change within themselves; a period which should be accepted as the natural thing that it is. By no means should it become one of embarrassment to the student. The most noticable change is in the voice of the student, particularily among the boys. It is not generally amusing to see the adolesent with his rapidly growing feet or lengthening legs; these things are accepted as a natural course of nature. But other parts of his body, such as the vocal chords are also growing. As these vocal chords grow there is a corresponding change in the voice, a condition often looked upon with amusement. When this growing change becomes apparent, it should be explained and discussed in the light of the production of musical sounds. The vocal chords are merely two muscles which we can control, separating them or bringing them together as we see fit. By forcing air between them they are caused to vibrate thus producing a sound. By a God-given gift we have learned how to make these sounds have a meaning; we have learned how to develop and control these muscles to such an extent that the tones produced may be very beautiful, and very accurate in pitch. The changing voice results from a lack of muscular control during the growing period. If, as these muscles grow, they become long and thick the voice will be lower and heavier; if they are short and thin the voice will be higher.

There is a need and a place for every voice be it high or low. As the young boy develops he goes through the stages of soprano, then alto-tenor—perhaps even the baritone. The period of this change is not long but it often covers a wide range of pitch and quality changes. This period, then, requires a gradual re-classification until the changing voice halts, becoming a tenor, baritone or bass. The change is not so noticeable among the girls but the final voice will rest either high or low and will be classified soprano or alto, depending on the color of the tone produced. There may be the *soprano* of high range, the mezzo-soprano of low range but soprano quality; there may be the *contralto* of high range of alto quality, or the contralto of low range with alto quality.

### The Senior High School

By the time the student reaches senior high school, he has probably settled on the logical and desirable instrument. He is now ready for an even greater concentration on his instrumental choice than he experienced in his junior high years. Vocally, the voice has become more settled in many cases and completely set in most cases.

In the high school, the student may find it necessary to choose between the vocal and instrumental phases of music. Some may find it possible and desirable to be active in both. Here, student guidance in music is needed so that the proper decision will be made. This guidance should be given honestly and in all fairness to the student, taking into consideration his possibilities in music and the good of the music organizations concerned. This guidance should also be in terms of the student's future vocation especially if the student has possibilities in the music field. For other students, the right use of leisure time can not be overly stressed and music should play a part in this.

Chapter XII

# THE DIRECTOR AS AN ORGANIZER

There are times when the music director is called upon to organize some phases of music promotion among which may be the festival, contest or clinic. Not all music directors are fortunate enough to go through this experience, but all should be acquainted with some of the working facts so necessary to a successful getting-together of music groups. If the director is acquainted with some of the problems and their solution, he or she will be more sympathetic toward those on whose shoulders rests the responsibility of such organization.

## The First Step

In the beginning, the host director must send out some form of an invitation together with some kind of an entry blank. This is necessary in order to have a basis on which to work. The next step is up to the probable visiting directors, to see that their application blanks are properly filled and invitations promptly accepted or rejected. With this answer in hand, the host director is in a position to start organizing.

## Selecting Judges or Clinitians

Unfortunately, the selection of judges or clinitians is too often tempered by the financial status of the host school. In any case, only the best available should be employed. While all-around musicianship is the paramount quality, judges should be placed so that they are judging that with which they are most familiar. While an instrumental man should judge an instrumental event better than a vocal person and the vocal event should be better judged by the vocally trained, there is no reason to believe that well schooled musicianship could do no other but good in either case. The matter of intonation, pitch, rhythm, attacks and releases, posture, smoothness, roughness and general effect are factors easily detected in any case by vocally or instrumentally trained persons.

## The Festival

If the planned meeting is of the Fesival type, there will probably be no limitation of the number to be present. This may take the form of a union of several bands, orchestras or choruses, or it may require only a few selected members from each. In the latter case, instrumentation and voicing must be considered since this is the usual plan for a clinic type festival. Sometimes, there are enough entrants to provide for more than one large performing group. In this case, plans must be made for a second or third group complete in every detail. Massed choruses of several hundred are much easier to control than are instrumental groups of similar size so it is better to have two bands, or orchestras of good instrumentation than to have one large un-wieldly group.

Sometimes, in dividing the group for a second or third band or orchestra, one organization is deliberately made up of superior musicians and the other made up of the less superior. This is not good psychological practice as it always promotes superior and inferior complexes among some young musicians. Also, two definitely different grades of music must be used and massed playing by the whole group will probably be on a lower level, if practiced at all. If the group is divided into organizations of nearly equal ability, the general playing and general effect will be much better, and massed performance becomes more nearly possible.

## Instrumentation and Voicing

As a rule, brass instruments are more readily available than are woodwind. For that reason the woodwind sections of band should be filled out before the brass instruments are added. In the orchestra, the full compliment of strings should be determined before the brass or woodwind are added. In this way proper balance can be preserved. In choral work, sopranos and basses are usually more numerous than altos and tenors, especially the latter. So, then, it will be better to build the size of the vocal performing group around the number of tenors available, knowing that even so there may be some necessary mis-proportion when adding the other four voices.

The number of persons acceptable for each section, vocal or instrumental, may be a problem. If this has not been pre-determined through consultation with other directors involved, the host director may consult any recommended list of band, orchestra or choral membership and multiply or proportion this accordingly.

If it is a matter of inviting bands of various sizes and abilities, instrumentation is not the prime worry since this can not be pre-determined or pre-set. In this case, the host director is concerned with supplying music of proper grade level for good massed performance. In the case of band, all percussion should be grouped together and preferably in the center front. In orchestra, the basses should be massed together as should all like voices accordingly in vocal groups.

## Housing

The housing problem often prevents the full expansion of a clinic or festival. Some schools have solved this by having their own students care for one or more of the visiting students during the period of the clinic or festival. In this case, breakfast is usually given by the host student—a courteous gesture of hospitality which may be eliminated easily enough if necessary. If this plan is used, it is best to have all visiting musicians assigned to homes before the day of the meet. The list of hosts and guests should be posted at an information desk where those concerned may get together.

## Seating the Musicians

The host director will be most concerned with the problem of seating the band or orchestra since these organizations have a tradition of first and second chairs to overcome. The choral groups are not so handicapped. The best method for seating is by actual tryouts with someone who understands the instrument in charge of each section. Scale passages may well show the technique, and there is nothing better than simple folk-like melodies to test phrasing, tone quality, interpretation and musicianship. A good and quick method is to have the players seated in one or more rows. Have the material for testing at hand, asking the first one to play the passage. Using this as a standard, have the second man play.

If he is better than number one, have him trade places with the first man. Then try the third one. If he is not as good as the second one leave him where he is. Try number four. If he is better than the third man let them trade places. This continues until the entire row has been tried. If this first test was for technique, let the second be for phrasing, interpretation and tone quality by using a well known folk tune. Again, shift the seating as merit demands. With little trouble, this will usually give a good picture of the best to the worst in order. Each section should understand that any seating arrangement is not permanent but is subject to change at any time.

In vocal groups, the arrangement will depend mostly on the appearance of the group when it is standing in performing position. Of course, in vocal groups there must be testing for voice ranges and voice quality which may well be done by sectional meetings.

### Rehearsal Planning

A complete schedule should be set up showing the time of rehearsals and the time allotment for each director who is to work with the group. The same procedure should be followed for sectional or instrumental rehearsals. Appropriate rest periods should be allowed but rehearsals should resume promptly on time.

### Entertainment

No group meeting is entirely complete without some form of entertainment for the visiting musicians where an overnight stay is necessary. Sometimes this is accomplished by a dance or party in the evening. This could, and should, be sponsored by the band parent's club or group of similar nature. Sometimes the local theatre will provide free admission for visiting musicians. Again, there are times when the local high school dramatics department will be presenting a play to which the students may be invited for one performance. A lyceum number could well be fitted into this by good planning previously. In any event, it is better to see that some form of entertainment is provided than to have a large number of young musicians roaming freely on the streets.

## Music

The problem of furnishing music need not be a difficult one even where the host school does not feel financially able to shoulder the cost. In such case, each visiting director may be asked to furnish the number or numbers which he or she wishes to direct. This solves the problem nicely, and at no cost. If the host school can borrow music from a neighboring college or university music department, so much the better but the host school should be prepared to pay for lost or damaged parts.

## The Contest

There is nothing more discouraging than a poorly organized music contest. The host director should take every advantage of all possibilities. First, lay out a plan showing where each event is to be held, the judge or judges for the event, and the time of starting. The starting time can be better determined after the total number of entrants is known. Usually five or six minutes are sufficient for solos, vocal or instrumental; ten minutes for the smaller ensembles and twenty minutes for choruses, glee clubs, bands and orchestras. If this time allotment is followed closely, there is little possibility of running behind schedule—a common fault in most contests.

Second, events of similar nature should not be scheduled at the same time. For instance, boy's solos should not be scheduled simultaneously with boy's quartets or boy's glee clubs. Schedule the boy's solos at the same time as the girl's solos or during the time when the girl's glee clubs or small ensembles are performing. If it is absolutely impossible to have this kind of schedule, then it is better to stagger the appearance of the large groups and the solos so that a soloist may appear early and the group with which he sings can perform later or vice versa. This will relieve congestion and confusion considerably.

## The Contest Manager

A third suggestion is that of having all rating sheets carefully and completely filled out before the day of the contest.

Each event should be presided over by a contest manager who should be provided with a large envelope on which is marked the name of the event, the hour, place, judge, contest manager and his helpers. The envelope should contain all the rating sheets necessary for that particular contest (these, the contest manager gives to the judge at the beginning of the contest) and a sheet showing the order of appearance of contestants, name of contestant and the town represented. The number showing the order of appearance must correspond with the number on the rating sheet for the same contestant.

The contest manager should keep the contest running smoothly, losing no time in calling each name in order. If one contestant does not appear at the proper time, the contest manager should go on to the next contestant. The one which did not appear at the properly assigned time may appear later if there is a lull, or perhaps wait until those who appeared in proper order have performed.

Those who are to help the contest manager should see that no one enters or leaves the room while a contestant is performing; that quiet maintains both in the room and near the doors, and be ready for any assistance which may arise in an emergency.

### Evaluating the Rating Sheets

All rating sheets should be relayed to one central point for evaluation and tabulation. The "runners" (those who collect and deliver the rating sheets) should be cautioned against giving out any rating information before it is officially posted on a bulletin board prominently located.

Each rating sheet should be signed by the judge and this should be insisted upon. If it is properly signed and marked then all information necessary to rating should be transferred to a master rating sheet. This sheet will contain the name of the event under which will be listed the name of the contestants, their school or town, and their rating.

Usually, one judge is used for the smaller events such as the solos and ensembles while at least three are, or should be, used for the larger groups such as chorus, glee club, band and orchestra. In the latter case, the final rating is the resultant of the three ratings. It is also good policy not to allow a conference between the three judges during the contest. The results and remarks should be the result of *three* hearings rather than a compromise. One judge should not know what the other judge has done or is doing. This makes for individuality in judging. Furthermore, the judges should be cautioned, in all cases, to write constructive criticisms only and to never criticize unless a remedy can be suggested. The criticism of a judge is of little value if the judge does not show how to overcome the fault or how to improve on the rendition. If he can not do this, the criticism should be left unwritten.

### Final Summary

From the master sheets giving the names of the events and the contestant ratings, the contest director should separate the contestants—placing each name and rating on another sheet set up for each town or school. In effect, the contest director started with the entry list from each town; he ends with a similar list for each town with the addition of the various ratings.

When the contest manager returns his envelope at the end of the contest, it should contain the list of contestants in order as originally given to which have been added notations concerning the non-appearance of any contestant. Some may withdraw by reminding the contest manager; some may not show up at all. In any case, proper notation should be made. In the final summary, then, this notation should be copied on to the proper rating sheet so that when the judge's rating sheets are returned to the various music directors, together with the rating sheet for their town, the director of music will be able to see the why and wherefore of each contestant which he originally entered.

### Final Gesture

The final gesture is payment of the judges. Usually, the total amount will include expenses such as travel, hotel and meals. If the latter may be had at the school cafeteria or lunch room there will be some saving. Sometimes judges may be housed in faculty homes. Sometimes during the day. a statement of the amount of expense incurred should be secured from each of the judges. This, together with the agreed fee, is the total expense and a check for this amount should be arranged for before the day is over—so the judge may leave with his pay. It is the courteous thing to do, and oftimes the judge relies on this for the return trip home. Also, prompt payment eliminates the possibility of misunderstandings through correspondence.

### Awards

Without a doubt, some form of achievement recognition should be given. Some contest directors still adhere to the giving of personal awards such as medals although there are some who believe this to be a necessary evil. The author holds to the latter view, believing that a printed card in certificate form serves the need admirably. Individual medals or cups are prohibitive where used in large numbers and the income is small. Perhaps such medals could be made availabble to those who are entitled to them by having the contestant pay the cost. The printed form may be had at a small cost and, when suitably framed, makes a very fine appearance on the wall of the music room. Medals usually end up in the dresser drawer.

### Aftermath

After the contest, the host director will always find copies of music left by various contestants and organizations. Other equipment such as music stands, instruments, music folders and even uniforms are sometimes left behind. These should be collected and sorted, sending each to its repective owner or school promptly. The music may be sent post-paid but the larger articles should be sent collect.

Chapter XII

SPORTSMANSHIP

The points in this book have been discussed with one thought in mind: to bring some of the things which go to make up a good musical organization to the attention of the music director. Fine qualities and faults of both the director and the organizations have been discussed but one more thing needs to be said: let us not part without a word on *sportsmanship*. If pitted against some other organization in a contest, festival, concert, parade or gridiron show, let the opposing organization be judged fairly but not harshly. Perhaps the other group is superior. If so, let it be recognized and steps taken to improve the situation so that at the next meeting this will not be true.

Too much time is often spent in finding fault rather than in finding corrections leading to improvement. Many alibis have been heard over the years and a careful tabulation reveals the following—all of them were, at some time, actually made by a music director:

1. The judges were crooked
2. Our uniforms were not good enough
3. We had too poor instrumentation
4. The judges didn't understand the composition
5. The judges didn't like our seating arrangement
6. The judges knew the other dircetor
7. Somebody told the judge to whom to give first
8. The judge was not listening when we played
9. I saw the judge talking to someone
10. The judge had a pupil in the other band, *I think.*
11. The other band marched on to the stage.
12. We didn't have an English horn
13. The whole contest was run crooked
14. We were all tired out
15. The judges were up all night before the contest

16. The band lost because we didn't do so well in the solo contests
17. We played last and the judges were all tired out
18. We played first and the judges weren't warmed up yet
19. They couldn't appreciate a good band
20. The judges wanted to pass around the first honors
21. Lost on account of a clarinet squeak
22. Cheering of the crowd swayed the judge
23. The winning director studied at the same university where the judge teaches
24. The judges were professionals and didn't understand education
25. Home crowd at the game too small to cheer for our band
26. Not enough loyal supporters
27. We did so much better at home, we just couldn't have done so bad here
28. We marched on from the wrong end of the field
29. Out of step? Ought to consider the age of my group
30. String bass fingering system? Is there one?
31. The judges were right—we simply weren't good enough

All these alibis, except the last, sound rather silly when put down on paper regardless of how serious they sounded when spoken. At best, alibis make a poor habit and a contagious one. When the director does it the habit soon filters down to the students and this makes for poor sportsmanship in the organization. The ideal combination would be a good organization plus good sportsmanship—win, lose or draw. In any case, a good loser is to be preferred over a poor winner.

Every music director has at some time been disappoined in the performance of his groups. The wise director has taken a careful inventory of the faults and made attempts toward correction—the poor director tries to find excuses for the showing. Similarily, the wise director will embark on a long-time program for his department and eagerly look forward to fine organizations in the near future, and then plan to keep them that way. The long-time program may be a three, four or five year plan and definitely some such plan should be inaugurated.

There is no chorus, band or orchestra equal to a *good* chorus, band or orchestra. The only way to develop such a fine organization is to teach properly the many little things which go to make up a creditable performance. Remember, a room is not swept unless the dust is out of the corners, neither is a circle round until it is of equal diameter in all directions. In other words, sweep out all the faults and an organization of perfection is in the making, an organization of which you, the administration and the community will be justly proud.

Chapter XIII

ELECTRONICS IN THE DIRECTOR'S WORK

The director of music should have some acquaintance with the field of electronics which is rapidly gaining a foothold in the field of music and has, in some instances, already become a necessity. Until the present time, the musician had to be content with what the ear heard when tuning his instrument In olden days it was instrument against instrument. Later there appeared the tuning fork which afforded a definite pitch, and man learned to listen to the "beats" (vibrations) as a means of tuning. Many years back, the tuning bar served the band and orchestra as a means of pitch guidance. This served a good purpose but the tuning bar was hopelessly limited to one note, leaving much to the assumption that if the instrument were in tune to concert A or B flat it would be in tune throughout its entire range. This not being true, the resourceful director soon learned to turn to the orchestra bells, and more recently to the vibraphone or vibraharp (without the vibrator) for tuning over a wider range.

Some directors have encouraged tuning *in reverse!* Instead of sounding the tuning-bell note and trying to match the tone with the instrument, the student sounds the note on his instrument and tries to make the bar of the vibraharp ring in sympahy. This will happen when the note on the instrument is played exactly in tune. Not only can this be done throughout the range of the instrument but it has the advantage of placing the emphasis on intonation through proper blowing rather than on the mechanics of the instrument.

### Electric Tuning Devices

Electronics means a change in tuning methods. There now appears on the market several devices for the tuning of an instrument through the aid of electricity. The types of machines vary from the instrument sounding a sustained tone of definite pitch to the one which reflects the tones of a full scale in the form of a graph.

The instrument sounding the sustained tone has the advantage of sufficient power to be heard by a group of almost any size and will sound either the tone of A or B flat. Here again is the same problem encountered in the use of the tuning bar: only *one* note is available for tuning. The second type of electric tuning instrument is equipped to reflect the tone, which is first played into a connected microphone, in the form of a graph which stands still if the tone is in tune, moves to the right if the tone of the player is sharp and moves to the left if the tone is flat. The decided advantage in this instrument is that a separate graph is available for each note of a complete chromatic octave. The disadvantage lies in its high cost. Schools not finding it possible to budget several hundred dollars for such a device may still have to contend with the tuning bar or the vibraharp.

### The Electric Organ

Some of the more fortunate schools have found it possible to add an electric organ to the array of musical instruments already owned. The electric organ serves as a wonderful background for a small orchestra such as might be used to furnish music for the stage show. Some directors not only use the electric organ as a harmonic instrument but have featured it as a solo instrument with band or orchestra in concert.

Should the purchase of an electric organ be contemplated, there are many choices as to manufacturer but only about three possibilities as to manner of tone production. One method uses a rotating disk set in front of a small magnet. The rotating disk, being of many sides (not perfectly round), sets up an electrical current through the magnet comparable to the number of sides on the disk. All disks rotate at the same speed on the same axle but the varying number of sides on the different disks makes various electrical impulses possible. These impulses are transformed into tones. In another method, the tone is produced by an oscillating tube—a more crude way of expressing it would be the harnessing of the radio squeal. The third type of tone productions picks up an electronic impulse directly from a vibrating reed set in motion by an air column much as the reed in the harmonica is set in motion. The sound of the reed is not amplified but the resulting electrical impulse is.

## Recordings and Recorders

Most school music departments own or have access to the standard recordings. A growing practice is to use recordings not only to illustrate the playing of the finest musical groups but to show the performance of the school organization itself. To do this, the music organizations make their own recordings which are played back to illustrate their own strong and weak points.

Several kinds of recording devices are available to the school music department. Where it is not possible to purchase a recording outfit for the exclusive use of the music department, perhaps it may be purchased as equipment for school-wide use. This would probably include the dramatics, English and other language departments along with music.

A most popular device is the wire recorder. This device picks up the sound through a microphone and transmits it to a moving wire. The wire, being sensitive to electrical impulses, retains the electrical pattern of the sound entering the microphone. By reversing the process, the recorded sound is returned through an amplifier and loud speaker. A similar device uses a paper tape instead of the wire. The advantage of these two types is that the wire or paper tape may be used over and over again by the simple process of de-magnetizing the wire or tape—a process mechanically done within the machine by the push of a button. The disadvantage is that the recording can not be retained for future playing if the wire or tape is to be used again. However, a library of wire or tape recordings can be built up if one buys additional reels of wire or paper tape.

The disk recorder serves best where the record is wanted for future playing reference. However, records come in six, eight, ten or twelve inch sizes and few school recorders are equipped to cut the large commercial records. The disk recorder has the advantage of recording at either 78 revolutions per minute or the slower speeds, either 33 1-3 or 45 revolutions per minute depending on the make. It is quite obvious that at the slower speeds about twice as much may be recorded as is possible at the speed of seventy-eight. It is also obvious that these slow recordings mut be played back at the same speed at which they were recorded. The merits of the most recent developments are yet to be determined.

The cost of each of the three types of recording machines, wire, tape or disk, is not high. There is little difference in cost of the wire or tape used but the cost of record blanks may run into a considerable amount, depending on the number of recordings made since a record blank can be used only once. The choice of types will be governed by the kind of service each can give.

### Recording and the Radio

In making recordings by school music organizations, the first few recordings will emphasize the fact that a new seating arrangement may be necessary if best results are to be achieved. The seating arrangement used for recordings will probably differ little from the arrangement used in broadcasting. It may be necessary to use the regular rehearsal room for recording or broadcasting, or perhaps the auditorium must be used. In either case, some experimentation will bring forth the most efficient seating arrangement.

It is not necessary for the school to have a broadcasting studio as such. A studio may be simulated very nicely, and at low cost. The size will depend on the room available and, again, it may have to be the regular rehearsal room. For better results the approximate relationship of height, width and length should be about 2 to 3 to 4 or 5. That is, for every two feet in height of ceiling, there should be three feet in width and four or five feet in length. Thus a room ten feet high, fifteen feet wide and twenty feet long would be in good proportion. However, this is not always possible and experimentation must again be the rule.

If possible, there should be a control room outside the room of performance. Where a room is not built for this purpose, the hall or an adjoining room may be used as a control room—signals to and from the director and engineer may be given through the glass door or window. Of course it is possible to leave the recording machine in the room of performance but this lessens the effect of having a performing studio and a control room.

There are various kinds of microphones in use and the local radio engineer or radio repair man should be consulted when this purchase is made. The microphone will be used either as a hand microphone or on a stand. In the latter position, it serves best for musical recordings and broadcasts. There are three types of microphones (1) the directional microphone which picks up from one direction only, the pick-up area spreading out from the microphone in fan shape, (2) the bidirectional which picks up from both sides and is most useful where a group is divided, and (3) the non-directional microphone which picks up from all directions at the same time reaching from itself in circular fashion.

## Vocal

Various vocal groups must be treated in different ways, final judgment coming from experimentation. If a quartet is used, each singer should be the same distance from the microphone for first experimentation. The voices should then be moved toward or from the microphone as seems suitable to a good balance. If head phones are available, the group can be heard just as they will sound on the recording or broadcast. The cost of headphones will be saved many times over in the pre-recording try-outs since each use of the head phones eliminates a practice recording.

Any voice which has a solo should be moved closer to the microphone, stepping quietly back into place when the solo is over. It should be remembered that all women's voices are lighter than those of men and should be closer to the microphone. As a rule the tenor voices of a male quartet, should be closer to the microphone. In the case of a mixed quartet, the male voices may better be in the center with the feminine voices on the outside.

Tremolo should be avoided as much as possible and in dramatic passages an increased intensity is preferred over singing louder. The best radio voice is not loud but is true, soft and clear, being as flexible as possible. In speaking and in singing, the S sound must be avoided as much as possible.

Where this is impossible, the S may become a part of the next syllable to be spoken if not overdone. All words should be spoken clearly and all syllables pronounced correctly.

The chorus or glee club will undergo some changes in voice arrangement but the general plan will follow that of the quartet in enlarged form.

## Instrumental

The use of instruments before the microphone is little different from the use of voices. Various instrumental groups require various seating arrangements. In most every case, the normal seating arrangement of the band or orchestra is insufficient for best recording or broadcasting.

The piano is probably the most commonly used instrument in radio or recording and considerable care should be taken to assure a balance between this instrument and other instruments or voices used with it. If the piano alone is used, the problem is lessened since only one tone is to be regulated. The lid of the piano may be raised or lowered, and the microphone may be near or far as the resulting sound requires. When other instruments or voices are used with the piano the microphone adjustment must be made so that the piano sounds as an accompaniment rather than as a solo instrument. It may be possible to use two microphones, one for the piano and one for the other instruments or voices with a panel mixing of the two. However, the common usage is that of one microphone unless the second is to be used for vocal or instrumental solo passages. Where only one microphone is used the solo voice must advance to the central microphone.

An instrumental quartet will probably achieve best results by using a bi-directional microphone as shown below, with a slight shifting of chairs to compensate for excessive carrying power of any one or two instruments:

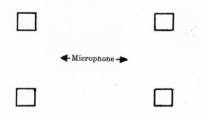

As the size of the performing organization is increased, it becomes necessary to devise other seating arrangements depending on the instrumentation and on the type of microphone used. Using a bi-directional microphone, the following arrangement may be quite successful, allowing, of course, for obvious instrumental variations, kind of microphone and studio dimensions:

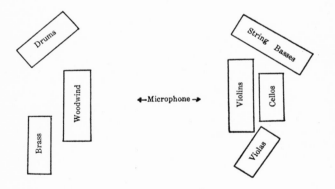

The above seating arrangement is in conjunction with a bi-directional microphone. With an unidirectional microphone the instruments will of necessity be placed on the live side of the microphone and some changes in seating positions must be anticipated. The following arrangement was used to good advantage in one instance with an unidirectional microphone:

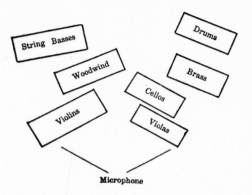

A seating arrangement for broadcasting a high school **band** known to have been quite successful follows:

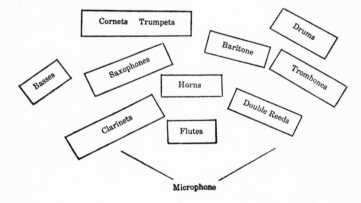

The above broadcasting was done with an unidirectional microphone.

The value of recording and radio broadcasting is no longer in the doubtful stage. The progressive and educationally mind-ed music director will make every effort to add as much of this equipment as is possible, starting perhaps with a wire or tape recorder since this device seems to be the most useful. However, this type of recording can not be of a permanent nature unless the director is prepared to tie up some of the departmental funds in extra reels of wire or tape which, fortunately, is not expensive.

It may be possible to build a considerable part of this equipment if there is a radio-minded student in the music department or school since the various parts of equipment may be purchased reasonably and a highly efficient recorder assembled.

Chapter XIV

## PUBLICIZING THE MUSIC

Publicity of the proper kind is necessary to the success of any musical venture where the public is to have a part either as a participator or as a listener. The problem which faces the music director is that of getting the necessary facts before the public in the most appealing way. Not all music directors have a gift for writing news but all directors have at their command the facts concerning the musical event to be presented. If the director can not write the news story himself, he should make every effort to organize the facts pertinent to the performance: what, where, when and who are the important questions to be answered in the news item. Once these facts are made known to the public, the musical program should be made to equal or surpass the publicity story.

### The School Paper

The school paper is the medium of publicity nearest the student body. It should be used not only to publicize the school music events but to keep the activity of the music department before the eyes of the student body. Strangely enough, the value of the school music program is too often measured by the amount of its activity. In fact, secondary school students want to have a part in music when they realize that something is always "going on". This curious fact also holds good for the adult.

### The Local Newspaper

The music director should avail himself of the benefits of the local newspaper, enlisting the support of this organ in his behalf at all times. The local paper is also eager to have news concerning the activity of the school music department because such items are usually "action" items. However, the music director should keep in mind that the editor has a "dead-line" for each issue and thus supply the publicity facts in plenty of time for the issue in which it should appear. If the local paper is a weekly one, usually a Thursday or Friday publication, the news should reach the editor not later than Wednesday morning, and Monday or Tuesday if at all possible. If the news is received by the editor in plenty of time he will give it a preferred place but when the publicity reaches him as late as Wednesday afternoon or Thursday morning it will have to fit in where ever possible, if at all. In addition, the editor will not be so eager to welcome further news if there is to be a corresponding inconvenience.

In the larger city the local paper is usually a daily paper but the desire to be of local service is still the objective. The city daily can be of considerable advantage to the town in the surrounding territory since a city daily is also eager to serve the metropolitan area which surrounds it.

### National Magazines

The music director should not overlook the value of state or national publicity for those events which are of more than local interest. Such state-wide magazines might be the official magazine of the state teachers association; the magazine supported by the state music organization; bulletins of the Federated Music Clubs, or bulletins supported by some of the larger music companies.

Many magazines cover a much wider territory than the state. These should be contacted where the news items would be of interest not only to those outside the immediate community but outside the state as well. Such information might cover the music camp activities, music festivals and contests especially those contests covering an area greater than the state.

### Local Clubs

The meetings of the various local clubs afford an excellent opportunity for announcements concerning the activities of the music department. Such local clubs will include the Chamber of Commerce, service clubs (Kiwanis, Lions, Rotary, Optomist and so on), study clubs and the Parent-Teacher Associations. In addition, the many local churches may cooperate in verbal announcements and bulletin notices.

Few meetings of the above fail to use music during their program, and all will have a period for any announcements of local interest. Talks emphasizing the value and importance of a good music program should be made before all of these clubs—and, if possible, in conjunction with a musical demonstration.

## Publicity Procedure

The music director should organize carefully the facts to be released in his publicity campaign. If he has no knowledge of writing news items for publication, he can at least develop an organized way of presenting the material to the editor or writers on the staff of he local paper. The local editors or writers on the staff of the local paper. The local out the necessary characteristics of good writing. First a statement should show what the music program is to be; its contents and purpose. After this, comes the date, the time and the place of performance. If room permits, the names of those participating should be included with a statement as to what part each plays. If there are committees active in the musical production, the names of members and their function should be given. Student assistants should be mentioned as should the accompanists. The director of music should not be too concerned that his own name appear in print yet he deserves credit for his efforts and should be so awarded. After all, publicity for the director is a part of his stock in trade and is valuable to him.

Pictures are not only of value but are a most desirable means of attracting attention. Action pictures are to be preferred over the posed type. Scenes from the operetta, the marching band, the chorus rehearsal, orchestral rehearsal, the student director in action, young musicians "wood-shedding" their parts, or music discussion groups, all are of value as *action* shots.

The use of cuts in the newspaper may require some additional cost to the paper or the school. If there is to be a choice between the school assuming the cost or not printing the picture, the advantage is in favor of the school paying for the cut. Oftimes one cut may serve the school paper, the local newspaper and some magazine of wider scope. In having the cut engraved, it is well to keep in mind the possible use of the cut since one most suitable to newsprint will not be suitable to glossy paper. The local newpaper or print shop can be a source of information as to the proper kind of cut to be made.

A careful survey of the music programs given from year to year will give the director a basis for a year's publicity. This will vary little, if any, from year to year. Most events will be repeated year after year, the only changes being in the names of those taking part. A survey will show certain seasonal programs throughout the year such as: Armistice Day, Thanksgiving, Christmas, Easter and National Music Week. These yearly events become rather standardized. Other music activities are continuous through the year and include concerts, church services, community activities, civic choral events, local fairs, athletic events, music contests. A few other activities may be classed as occasional or special events. These may include out-of-town programs, booster trips, choir festivals, civic drives and music festivals.

By organizing the year's program, the music director is better able to organize his publicity material, rewriting material used the year before making changes where necessary. Many directors keep a folder of publicity material, a folder containing the coming events in order of appearance with all possible facts pertaining to each. The year's program may appear as a bare outline in September but as the time for the various events approaches, there is a gradual filling in of the necessary publicity material.

One last thought may be of value. Study the news stories released by other schools as printed in the papers in surrounding towns. All newspapers have an exchange with other papers and these are available for reading. Considerable knowledge of news writing may be gained from this source; it is certainly worth the effort if the director feels he is lacking in this phase.

Chapter XV

## ODDS AND ENDS

In reading the preceding chapters, there comes to mind many odds and ends which seem to fit in no particular chapter but which merit some attention and discussion. Perhaps whole chapters could be written on each subject and, indeed, some authors have given considerable space to each. Here, the music director will be reminded of some important items along with the suggestion that further reading of supplementary material will be of great benefit.

### The Library

One of the necessary reqirements of equipment is the music library. The possibility of acquiring a music library is dependent upon the economic conditions under which the director has to work. He may be allowed a specific amount for music, or he may depend on donations or money raised by school events. The director who must depend on individual student-purchase of parts is indeed handicapped. He is apt to have few numbers with complete instrumentation for as the students graduate, the library (or parts of it) oftimes graduate with them. Where individuals of the musical organization purchase the music, there is generally some problem in checking on separate parts unless the number becomes a real and definite part of the school music library.

Where the organization depends on civic help such as may come from parent's clubs, a definite library goal may be set up but this help is some reflection on the ability of the school to finance its own organization.

Whatever the method of obtaining a music library, a more important point is how to *retain* it. There are various ways of checking and taking care of the library. Obviously, there must be a safe and sure way to get at the music before it is used and, in turn, a safe and sure way of getting it back to its proper place after it has been used.

Seldom does a band or an orchestra fail to use folders, the only safe and sane way to handle music in rehearsal. Each folder should be identified in some manner. Some directors use a letter to designate the folder such as using the letter A for violins, B for violas, C for Cellos. D for string bass, E for oboe, F for flute and so on through the list of orchestral groups. A similar plan may be used for band. Each piece of music should be marked with a letter which coincides with the letter on its folder. Another plan is the use of numbers in place of the letters.

A third plan of identification is the use of instrumental names and numbers, as:

> Oboe I
> Oboe II
>
> Flute I
> Flute II
>
> Clarinet I
> Clarinet II
> Clarinet III
> Clarinet IV

Each piece is then numbered to correspond with the folder number, the folder number corresponds to the stand in its section thus clarinet IV means the folder for the fourth stand of clarinets. This method is a very simple one and is easy both for the director and the student librarian, the latter also being a necessary part of the director's library set-up.

The most acceptable place for keeping the band, orchestra or choral music is in fire resisting cabinets. If these are not available, then some sort of cabinets or shelving should be built which will allow easy access to all music. The library should be indexed and cross filed for quick reference. This is especially true for the large library. A small library need not be so kept if the library work is done by the director and he is thoroughly acquainted with the manner in which it is filed.

Where the library is indexed and cross-filed, the first filing should be by title, second by composer, and finally by type although every director may have his own opinion as to the relative importance of the order. The director may desire a further break-down in cross filing.

Some directors find it advantageous to use index cards of various colors, each representing one file such as white for title, blue for composer etc. Such color arrangement prevents any error in card filing.

The vocal music library presents fewer problems than does the band and orchestra music since the great majority of numbers used will be for four parts. This makes the laying out and sorting of music much easier than where one must work with twenty or thirty parts as in band and orchestra. In vocal groups, no less than one folder for each two singers should be provided and preferably one folder for each singer although this doubles the cost of music. One copy for each singer is prohibitive for most schools and is unwise in the light of the fact that two numbers may be purchased for the cost of one where one copy serves two people.

Choral folders should be identified by number or letter and each selection marked to correspond with its folder number. This helps in tracing lost parts especially if each pair of singers are assigned a definite folder. The choral music should be catalogued and cross indexed for quick reference and better service.

## The Student Director

The director should not overlook the possibilities of a student director. From the standpoint of time saved and actual added help in rehearsal and performance, the student director has considerable value to say nothing of the advantage to the student.

Better organizations can be built by encouraging student directors. Student directing gives the young musician an insight to the problems which confront the director, and it teaches the young director the value and necessity of full co-operation of everyone in the group. This knowledge filters through to those musicians who are not student conductors and coming from the students themselves, the idea of co-operation has no taint of teacher propaganda. Lastly, the student director is impressed with his musical responsibility to the group and to the community. Some may want to become teachers of music. For those who do, this training is an excellent background for later work in college. For those who do not, the training is an excellent thing musically.

For the good of the school music organization, the student director is the logical helper to the director and should be subject to call many times. For this reason, the director will exercise great care in selecting his student director. He may have a class in conducting, selecting the most likely student from this group or he may simply pick some young student who seems to have possibilities. The student should be chosen because of his interest and sincerity in music, for his ability to lead the group, and for his knowledge of music. The student director will, in many cases of necessity, act in place of the director and should, therefore, have many of the qualities needed in a good director. The student director might be required to carry on so many rehearsals per semester, check and criticize a certain number of solos, supervise some sectional rehearsals, etc. Of course the director must always be in the background but the approach used by the student director should not be that which causes resentment among other players or singers. The student director will have what authority is necessary but must not make too much use of it. If the student director program can not be so organized then it had better be omitted. It may either be an advantage or a detriment, and only the former should be tolerated.

The director who finds it possible to have a class in conducting will probably have a class of earnest music students who desire to become music directors. For this reason the time of class meeting is of little concern. It may be held before school or after school and, being an elective class, the ordinary discipline problems are absent. It may be possible to have a conducting class during the school day, and possibly it might be incorporated in the school music program.

There are many things a director will want to include in his student directing course. These vary from the physical set-up of chairs for rehearsal to the actual conducting of a final performance .The simple movements of beating time are essential but these are not all which must be taught. The student conducting class must include all the major and minor details which confront the director in his daily work. The student director should have a good knowledge of the music library. He should know the use and kind of various instruments in band and orchestra and voices in the chorus, and the seating arrangement necessary for the group. With some basic background, he is ready for lessons in beating time. This may be done with the aid of recordings (especially those of the school music organizations) or with the piano.

As the class grows in knowledge and experience, it can serve the school well by assisting in music testing programs, sectional rehearsals, training of younger groups, and in actually taking over the better school music organizations.

### Popular Music

Few music directors have not faced the question of using popular music, especially is this true of the band and the chorus. The concert orchestra is less susceptable to this for it enjoys immunity by long years of tradition. In addition, there are few orchestrations of popular music suitable for use with a concert orchestra whereas it is quite common for band and chorus. There are some very nice arrangements too, for the band and the chorus. At times the band can use swing versions to advantage and although many do not believe in it there is a great amount of training to be found in the use of popular arrangements especially in rhythm patterns. In using popular music, the director should not make the mistake of accepting a low standard of perfection. Apparently many directors feel that the standard of perfection need not be high when using popular music. This is what makes the playing of popular music sound so bad by so many organizations, they accept a low standard. Popular music is not easy to play well and the director should require the same degree of perfection that he would of any other concert number.

The chorus has not fallen for this low standard of popular music production as has the band. Beautiful voices are at their best in the long accepted choral numbers of Palestrina and Bach style, but the value of the chorus to the school would be limited indeed if this type of music were used to the exclusion of all else. Some directors are organizing swing choirs as a division of their larger choral groups. Invariably, they select their better voices because of the realization that only the better voices can do justice to popular music. May the day come when the band director arrives at this same conclusion. Many a popular number has been played with careless abandon by the band with no near approach to the proper rhythm patterns nor even the proper pitch sometimes and this to an extent which the director would never tolerate in a concert number or even in the more common march.

In any event, the wise director will select popular music suitable to the occasion, submerging self prejudice to the need of the hour. If the organization is a good one, well trained in playing and singing fundamentals and brought up with a decent approach to, and appreciation for, music, there will be no harm done by playing popular music—and in practically all such cases the students come to know popular music as one small phase of a very great music field but certainly not the paramount phase.

## Choosing A Contest Number

Whether the music contest has a certain required number or not, there is still the necessity for choosing at least one number especially suitable to the performing group. Most contests have one required number plus a selected number; other contests allow only the selected number; in any case there is also a march to be selected where the band participates. So, the director is faced with finding a number suitable to his performers. The only way to do this is to choose that number which will show off your musicians.

Instrumentally if the brass section is strong but the reeds are weak then choose a number favorable to the brass—a flashy, brilliant type of number will fit admirably. If the entire band is weak in instrumentation then the number should be well cross-cued. If the trombones are strong then look for a number with considerable melodic work for this section. The same would be true for baritones or basses. Examine the number to see how strong and important are the inner parts especially the horns and the lower voiced reed instruments. If the basses and baritones seem better than the rest of the band then select something with plenty of bass runs and bass solos with a supporting accompaniment of horns and cornets especially. This, plus the woodwind and trombones, should afford a good contrasting background.

If the required number happens to be all out of line with the instrumentation which must be used, the director can certainly do some retrieving through a well selected number. This applies to the so-called warm-up march. The wise director will not only select this march very carefully but will spend considerable time on it in rehearsal. It is the first thing heard by the judges and it is almost impossible to keep him from making mental notes of it and the author has never received a returned contest adjudication sheet which did not contain the judging of the warm-up march.

One of the greatest drawbacks of the contest is the limitation placed on the repertoire of the musical organization. Generally, the system is that of several acceptable numbers of which the director must choose *one*. This makes it possible for the director to know early in the school year at least one of the numbers he will use in the Spring contest. He will probably spend most of the year with this number in rehearsal. This is neither healthy nor the original idea of a selective list.

The real fault lies in the fact that few directors and administrators are willing to forego the chances of *winning* just one year in order to teach a few good fundamentals of music with good sight reading being the object. It would be far better to not participate for a year or so and build a better musical organization than to rehearse all year on two contest numbers to *win* a contest. The true test of any musical organization is its ability to use the known music fundamentals. Too many music organizations, after a year's practice on two numbers, can win a contest but can't play "Home Sweet Home" at sight.

A good rule to follow in selecting music for the chorus is to carefully read through each of the various parts. If the director can read the parts readily and easily, the chances are the chorus can sing the number. However, if the director can not read the separate parts he should not expect his chorus to do so. The placement of voices should be reasonable, each part singing within its own range with no sudden or awkward jumps to an extremely high or low register. The melody should run along smoothly with natural, easy accompaniment parts. If there is to be any skipping, it should be in the bass part preferably.

### Sight Reading

The real musical test of an organization be it vocal or instrumental is its ability to sight read and no experience illustrates the true type of music teaching as does that of sight reading. Certainly, teaching how to *use* the fundamentals of music in actual participation should not be sacrificed at the expense of playing pieces. Any director with a good conception of the number he is to use in concert or contest may go through every part, marking everything such as expression, dynamics, holds, ritards, etc., and soon have his students performing it perfectly in a mechanized way. An organization so trained may have complete unity on the pieces so learned but when they attempt sight reading they have no red and blue pencil marks, various indications are not outlined or underscored, there is no guide and the organization becomes lost for it has been taught not music reading, not to use the fundamentals of music but only to perform in a parrot-like manner. The true test of musicianship is sight reading and the true test of solo singing or playing would be a performance without accompaniment.

The best way to learn to sight read is to sight read. Organizations which have done little sight reading should read slowly at first, making sure that the first beat in each measure is emphasized. The music should be thought of as perpendicular rather than horizontal. In other words, keeping track of the beat is fundamental as is good attention to the chord progression. Re-statement of themes should be recognized and emphasized, and the correctness of intervals should be stressed. In all, good sight-reading calls for careful attention and quick adjustments to such changes as pitch, rhythm, key and time signatures, intervals, measure values and accidentals, all of which are merely the fundamentals so necessary in the beginning training period.

## School and Community

Books could be written about the responsibility of the school program to the community so only one bit here: of what value is all our extended school music program if it does not benefit the community as a lasting thing? Winning a prize or contest is a temporary thing. So is the occasional concert or program. The permanent thing would be an infusion of music into the lives of the school students to such an extent that their musical experiences would not end with graduation. The school music program should overflow into a community program not only in the form of a community band and orchestra but as a community chorus, and in the form of many community ensembles. The music director should have this under his direction and include it in his plans and, of course, should be paid in proportion to what this enlarged plan is worth to the community.

Instead of using the junior high and grade years as a training period for the senior high organizations, the whole school program—elementary and secondary—should be the training period for greater community living through music. While the same thing could be done through dramatics, the opportunities for community-wide programs in music can not be excelled.

## Bibliography

Finally, let it be stated that no one book can adequately cover a subject since every author has his own methods of approach. The school music director should have available, either in his own library or the library of the school or city, many books on the various phases of school music teaching so that his own background will be neither narrow nor biased. The following list of books afford a wealth of supplementary reading material.

## ACOUSTICS

*Acoustics of Music,* Bartholomew, Prentice-Hall
*Musical Acoustics,* Culver, Blakiston

## CONDUCTING

Essentials in Conducting, Gehrkens, Oliver Ditson
The School Music Conductor, Wilson-Bodegraven, Hall-McCreary
Handbook on Conducting, Scherchen Oxford Univ. Press
The Baton in Motion, Otterstein, C. Fischer, Inc.
Expressive Conducting, Krone, Kjos
The Man with the Baton, Ewen, Crowell

## GENERAL

Twentieth Century Music, Bauer, Putnam
The Key to the Art of Music, Howes, Crowell
Music and Criticism, French, Harvard Univ. Press
The Shaping Forces in Music, Toch, Criterion
The Common Sense of Music, Spaeth, Garden City
The Book of Musical Documents, Nettl, Philosophical Library

## INSTRUMENTAL

The Concert Band, Goldman, Rinehart and Co.
Instrumental Music in the Public Schools, Norman, Oliver Ditson
Practical Problems in Building Wind Instruments, C. G. Conn, Ltd.
Orchestration, Forsyth, MacMillan
Getting Results with School Bands, Prescott and Chedister, C. Fischer and P. A. Schmidt
Modern Instrumentation for Modern Arranging, Jones, J. P., W. C. Brown
Success in Teaching School Orchestras and Bands, Righter, P. A. Schmidt
Building the Instrumental Music Department, Jones, L. B., C. Fischer, Inc.

## MUSIC EDUCATION

Education for Musical Growth, Mursell, Ginn and Co.
Music Education Source Book, Morgan, MENC

*Learning Music Through Rhythm,* Hood-Schultz, Ginn and Co.

*Psychology of Music,* Seashore, McGraw-Hill

*Music Education in the Elementary School,* Brooks and Brown, American

*Creative School Music,* Fox and Hopkins, Silver-Burdett

*Music Teaching in the Elementary Grades,* Hubbard, American

*The Teaching and Administration of High School Music,* Dykema and Gehrkens, Birchard.

## SHOWMANSHIP

*Building A Show Band,* Wettlaufer, Belwin, Inc.

*Band Pageantry,* Bergan, Remick

*Gridiron Pageantry,* Righter, C. Fischer, Inc.

*Parade Technique,* Johnson, Belwin, Inc.

## VOCAL

*The Chorus and its Conductor,* Krone, Kjos

*Vocal Technic,* Tkach, Kjos

*Read This and Sing,* Dengler, John Church

*The Living Voice,* Wilcox, C. Fischer, Inc.

*Choral Arranging,* Wilson, Robbins

### Conclusion

As prophesied in the beginning, the fore-going has been no attempt to establish any particular method or manner of teaching school music. Rather, it has been simply a bit of retrospective thinking about a number of factors so vital to the production of good music. Many of these factors are recalled from actual experience in school music teaching; others have come from friendly directors who have shared their musical experiences, good and bad. From these same sources have come the remedies suggested.

It is readily admitted that all possible situations have not been discussed, nor was there any attempt to do so. New and unexpected situations will arise constantly and only an adaptation of some past solution will meet the need. Constant reference to good books will be of considerable help. This is the reason for the inclusion of the above bibliography which the author has found both interesting and helpful reading. The music director should subscribe to those nationally known music magazines which best suits his needs; he should build a personal library not only of books but of magazines as well. The director of music should take an active part in the district and state music education associations. By all means. this activity should be extended to the national music organization.

A successful director of instrumental music once remarked that producing a fine band or orchestra is really a simple matter, requiring only that the notes be played properly. While the actual production of music may not be quite so simple there is considerable truth in the statement. The music director is concerned with the process or processes required "to play the notes properly." It behooves the music director to reinforce his present knowledge with much study through reading and association with other teachers of school music. The academic training period in college is only a background which must be supplemented by the director's own efforts.

This book makes no attempt to set forth new and radical ideas but there is a hope that in reading it the reader has been provoked to some thought on improving his work and that there has been kindled a re-newed interest. If this has come about. the author has been more than well paid.